W9-ANI-887

Cleveland is a city of paradoxes. It is a sprawling modern
metropolis, and a small town as well. It was founded by New England
Protestants, but it is now peopled by ethnic groups
from every corner of the world. It supports the nation's
most elegant cultural complex, and a host of blue- collar,
shot and beer neighborhoods.

Whatever Happened to the "Paper Rex" Man?

is a collection of short essays about the Near West Side
of Cleveland. Informative, charming and nostalgic, they reflect
the paradoxical nature of their neighborhood as it evolved
over 100 years. Included are vignettes of big businesses like
Joseph and Feiss and smaller ones like the Broken Cookie Store;
great churches like St. Patrick's Bridge and the storefront
churches of ethnic groups emerging in the 1950s; giant operations
like the old stockyards, and the legendary "umbrella man."
All in all, the collection is a gem; sure to bring a tear to
the eye of anyone reminiscing about the "good old days" of
Cleveland's Near West Side.

Norman Krumholz, *Professor, Cleveland State University*

WHATEVER HAPPENED TO THE "PAPER REX" MAN

WHATEVER HAPPENED TO THE "PAPER REX" MAN

and Other Stories of Cleveland's
Near West Side – 20th Century

THE MAY DUGAN CENTER CLEVELAND, OHIO 1993

COPYRIGHT 1993
by The Near West Side Multi-Service Corporation
D.B.A. The May Dugan Center

All rights reserved. This book or any part thereof may not be
reproduced in any form whatsoever, whether by graphic, visual,
electronic, filming, microfilming, or any other means, except in the
case of brief passages embodied in critical reviews and articles,
without the prior written permission of the publisher.
Write to:

DIRECTOR
MAY DUGAN CENTER
4115 BRIDGE AVENUE
CLEVELAND, OHIO
44113

(216) 631-5800

Library of Congress No. 93-084090

ISBN: 0-96307-6019

Second Printing, July, 1993

THE enclosed vignettes tell the stories of many parts of life in the Near West Side of Cleveland, Ohio, during the 20th century. They are written by many people with the hopes of recording memories of a fascinating part of history where the American lifestyle experienced enormous change and growth.

They are here for the reader to get a glimpse of tradition that can't always be found in history books, and will, hopefully, be passed down to another generation to better understand the development of humankind.

This booklet was inspired by the Near West Side Hometown Club, a development of the May Dugan Center.

ACKNOWLEDGEMENTS

Coordinating a book of thirty-three (33) writers was a challenge in itself, but it never would have been possible without some special people.

John Szilagyi, director of the Community Graphics Program at the Cleveland Institute of Art, gave us much encouragement and patience as he and his students worked on the book design. Many people phoned or wrote when they heard about the book and their enthusiasm pushed us to complete it. Others agreed to let us interview them to share data. Typists Rebecca Toney, Julie Southworth and Josefa Ramirez typed numerous drafts. Proof readers, Mary Englert and Fred Pizzedaz, tried to catch most of our typos and context problems. The Near West Side Hometown Club gave us the initial inspiration. The John P. Murphy Foundation and Forest City Enterprises Charitable Foundation helped us financially to accomplish this first printing. The many writers believed in the Near West Side of Cleveland.

To all of these people, we are deeply grateful.

We dedicate this book to future generation Near West Siders.

CONTRIBUTING
WRITERS:

Tom Andrzejewski
Gabor S. Brachna
Alice Butts
Grace Campbell
Jim Chura
Marnie Fell Cravens
Natalie Cravens
Helen DiBin
Mary Englert
Holly K.Gigante
Joan Dunn-Gill
Hildegarde Gorman
Terry Hayes
Maryanne Henderson
Mary Hillman
Bill Jenks
George M. Keith

V.A. Kilbane
Fr.Tom Mahoney
Barbara McMahon
Mary Kay McManamon
Paula Margoci-McClain
Margaret Middleton
Patricia Ehlen Milenius
Sylvia Paul
Garry Roggenburk
Carol Sabo
Paul Sabo
Margaret Simmerly
Mary Conway-Sullivan
Norman Thorne
Rebecca Toney
Cindy Ward

CONTENTS

Really–Where is The Near West Side? 13

Bakeries 14

Whiskey Island:
    The Island That Isn't There 15

A Potpourri of Memories 17

Cleveland Sandlot Baseball 18

What We Did For Fun 20

Rubbish Pickin' 21

The Gordon Neighborhood 22

Winter Fun 23

Rollercade 24

Early Nineteenth Century Immigrants'
    Contribution to the City Of Cleveland 26

A Man to Remember 28

Early 1900's 30

"Paper Rex" Man 31

West Side Memories 32

James Ford Rhodes 33

West Side Community House 34

Day Care Baby 35

Pizza, Potato Chips, Ice Cream, –
    Back When 38

The Corner Store 39

Abbey Market 40

Penny Candy 42

John Patrick "Johnny" Kilbane 45

Rail Transportation 46

Alleys 47

Street Scenes 48

Bridges 49

Stockyards 50

Drugstores 51

Breweries 52

Some West Side
    "Good Old Days" Reflections 53

Out To Eat 55

To Market To Market 56

Joseph and Feiss Company 59

The Heisman House(s) 60

Teachout House 61

Lost in the 50's 63

Gone Fishin' 64

Orchard School 66

Door Service 67

Second Empire Italianate 68

William L. Halloran 70

The West Side Hungarian
    Lutheran Church 71

Pops 73

A Former St. Ignatius H.S. Student
    Remembers the Past 74

Harry O 76

I Could Have Danced All Night 77

1950's Music 78

1956 79

Cudell 80

Memories of Greenwood 82

Neighborhoods: Mid-Century 83

Old Movie Theaters on the West Side 84

Summer in the City 86

Housing Along the Lake 87

Coming of Age 88

It wasn't Club Med 89

Looking Back 90

Shopping 91

Some Hard Ways 92

Broken Cookie Store 93

Churches – A Legacy of Cultures 94

"Solid As A Rock" 96

Memories of Youth 97

My Life On The Near West Side 99

St. Stephen School Days 100

St. Patrick's – Bridge 101

St. Colman 102

St. Mary's On-The-Flats 104

Miles of Walking 105

The Old Neighborhood 106

A Special Club –
   A Special Place and Time 107

CSU – CLEVELAND PRESS ARCHIVES

❧

REALLY —
WHERE IS
THE
"NEAR
WEST SIDE?"

Many people say it reaches from the "Boulevard" (W. 102nd) to the River; and from the Lake to what is now Denison Avenue. But it wasn't always like that. The development of the Near West Side began a long time ago, when, in 1807, pioneer families, the Lords and the Barbers came from the East Coast to the area as investors in what some say was one of the biggest real estate deals ever.

The Lords and Barbers were part of a group of early settlers who bought the right to own land in the Western Reserve, which was then owned by the state of Connecticut. The Western Reserve stretched from the Pennsylvania border 120 miles West to the area near Sandusky between Lake Erie on the North and the area just South of Akron and Youngstown.

Together, this group of investors put up over one (1) million dollars —a huge amount of money back then. Each investor was given the chance to obtain plots of the land through a drawing in April, 1807. The Lords and Barbers pulled the largest parcel, which stretched from the Cuyahoga River to West 117th and from Lake Erie to Brookpark Road, naming it Brooklyn Township.

These pioneers had the land surveyed, and in 1836, further incorporated an area from the Cuyahoga River to West 58th Street, from Lake Erie to Walworth Run, near the present day rapid tracks. They called this area the City of Ohio. The center of the City of Ohio was called Market Square, and it extended from W. 25th to West 38th Street. The turnpike (what we now refer to as Pearl Road or West 25th Street) was the main road in the area.

Until 1854, the City of Cleveland and the City of Ohio were totally separate. In June of 1854, the City of Ohio and some of the area surrounding it was annexed to Cleveland. It then grew to become known as the Near West Side of Cleveland.

More recently, other kinds of "labels" have been given to divisions of Cleveland's lands. The Strategic Planning Areas (SPAs) define areas one way; the police districts another; and the City Council yet another.

Many "regular" people don't use any of these categories when they say where they live or work — they just say "around such and such street," or the near west end.

Overall, we consider the Near West Side as the part nearest the Cuyahoga River, out west to about the Boulevard, and from the Lake south to Denison

– Patricia Ehlen Milenius

13

BAKERIES

There's nothing quite like waking up in the morning to the sweet smells of baking bread. What's even better is to smell it, all over your neighborhood, as you trudge off to work or school. Fresh baking bread provided a silent kind of "soul" to the neighborhoods of the West Side throughout the first half of the 20th Century.

There were the "huge" baking companies. Laubs, dating back to 1889, was on Lorain and W. 50th. It was the first to sell sliced bread, and boasted, in the early 50's as the nation's largest home-delivery baking company, employed over 400 employees. Spangs began on Barber, in 1888, and grew with an outlet on Lorain and one in Akron. It, too, employed over 400 people into the 50's. Farther west, you couldn't help but catch the winds of N.B.C., located by Western and 110th. These big baking companies baked white bread, rye, potato; rolls, biscuits, cakes, whatever. Mostly, they sold to stores and delivered their goods directly to neighborhood homes, by trucks. You always knew when the bakery truck was coming—once, twice a week down your street, you'd hear the bell ringing. Back then, you could pay the bakery man right away, or you could put the charges on your "tab" and catch-up the following week.

That's the way it was.

There were also the smaller bakeries, dotted all over the West Side, many reflective of the particular neighborhood nationalities. Everything was homemade with the finest ingredients — custard biscuits, ladylocks, cinnamon buns, kolachi, pecan rolls, raisin bread, different ryes, hard rolls, cracklin biscuits, housky, donuts, cream puffs, eclairs, jelly rolls. It was a delight just looking through the glass windows, trying to make up your mind.

And the bakers, with towels often draped around their necks and flour dust on their arms, knew the people by name or face. Whether it was Mary's on 25th, or Busby's on 31st, Marvin's on W. 41st, or Mazzones on Clark, or Kaase's on 29th, Jirik's on Storer, Halasy's on 98th—these bakers were a genuine part of the neighborhoods, and took great pride in their work and the happiness it brought their customers.

– H.K.G.

WHISKEY ISLAND: THE ISLAND THAT ISN'T THERE

Whiskey Island is an island that isn't there, in the heart of swamps that no longer exist. Its 22 streets have virtually disappeared, along with all the housing that sheltered its onetime bustling population. The people are long gone too, together with the 13 saloons they once kept in business.

Nonetheless, this island of memories still lies on Cleveland's doorstep, just west of the entrance to the Cuyahoga River. It's actually a triangle-shaped peninsula, with its base measuring a mile along the shore of Lake Erie. It measures a third of a mile at its widest point, from north to south, which is about half way between the banks of the Cuyahoga River and West 54th Street.

In the 17th Century, the "island" was home to Erie Indians. At that time, it was the only solid ground in the area, for everything else was nothing but swamp for about three-quarters of a mile upriver. That was the way Moses Cleaveland found it in 1796. Lorenzo Carter, the first settler, made it his farm and put in a still at the eastern end. Hence the name Whiskey Island.

According to journalist William F. Hickey, in his contribution to Cleveland State University's Ethnic Heritage Studies, the knoll had been called Whiskey Island years before the Irish arrived, "but if it hadn't been, it would have had to have been renamed."

Hickey wrote that the "brawny diggers who survived the poverty, pestilence and ostracism they encountered at every turn...through sheer grit and a laugh here and there, established the Irish beachhead on the shores of Cleveland...May all their shovels rest easily..."

The Irish, who had earlier dug the Erie Canal, came in the late 1820's and early 30's to do the digging for the rechanneling of the Cuyahoga River from an outlet near Edgewater Park to its present location. Since Cleveland's Yankee population numbered only about 1,000 at the time, the 200 hardfisted laborers had quite an effect on the community.

They lived in shanties at first, struggling to survive exploitation by their employers and a killing outbreak of cholera. According to the Encyclopedia of Cleveland History (Van Tassel & Grabowski, 1987), the city's second hospital, the "pest house," was built on Whiskey Island in 1832. However, the Irishmen's numbers doubled to about 400 during that decade, when an economic boom produced docks and some manufacturing plants on the island. And the number of Irish women increased, usually sisters of the diggers who sent passage money.

Work on the docks and industry in the Flats, together with the famine in Ireland, brought thousands more Irish immigrants to Cleveland during the remainder of the century. But human living on Whiskey Island gradually eroded as the people moved through and upward out of the Flats, chiefly onto the West Side.

They were replaced by railroad facilities, iron ore, hoisting machines, a salt mine, warehouses and storage tanks. Many of these you can see from the West Shoreway or Detroit Avenue. Next time you pass by, listen carefully. Maybe, out of the past, you'll hear the faint sounds of Erie Indian chant or Irish laughter and song.

– Mary Englert

PHOTO: COURTESY RALPH ABRAHAM

A
POTPOURRI
OF MEMORIES

Sylvia Paul was born in March of 1899 on Prague Avenue, off West 65th St. Delivered by a midwife, she was the last of ten children born to immigrant Czech parents. Her fondest personal memory was being part of a World Championship girls' basketball team, coached by a Mr. Kemeny. At 92, she also recollects:

> Living in the Stockyard District where rabbis came to slaughterhouses to kill the animals with knives. The Jewish faith believed meat could not be eaten unless the animal was killed this way. Theurer-Norton Provision Co., Swift & Company, Bloomenstock & Reid were a few of the area meat companies near the Big 4 Railroad Tracks at W. 61st and Clark...
>
> Watching the horse-drawn brewery wagons from Pilsner Brewery, at 65th and Clark, and Standard Brewery on Train, pass on the street...
>
> Going to the outhouse in your backyard. Most were partially surrounded by holly-hocks and sunflowers, cleaned once a week, had a Sears Catalog for toilet paper and once every several months were cleaned out by men with large barrels. They were called "honey dumpers"...

> You'd shop at Waibels Hardware (where Sylvia bought her first stove for $39.50 in 1924), Bonakers Chocolate & Ice Cream Parlor, Gideon's Grocery and Dry Goods, Klein's Blacksmith and Carriage Shop (there weren't many cars around in the early 1900s), Walters Florist Shop, Kocian's Bake Shop, Tausus Jewelry Store (Mr. Tausus was killed when the Lusitania sank)..
>
> Meier's Victrola Store, and Jirik's Bakery (known for their famous housky). Schmotzers shoes had walls covered with shoes from the floor to the ceiling. They had a ladder with wheels and a rail at the top to glide across it —so from top to bottom — the shoes you wanted to see were easy to reach ...
>
> You'd go to the National Theatre for a movie, to the Hungarian Gardens for dances, watch a prize fight at Storer & W. 63rd, visit Lutz's bowling alley or Brookside Park, for swimming or the zoo. Many churches held picnics at a large field (called Big Creek) by W. 56th and Denison...
>
> You'd get paid 10 cents/hour and could rent a house for $5/month...

Such were sweet memories that spanned almost a century of life in the Near West Side.

– *Rebecca Toney*

CLEVELAND
SANDLOT
BASEBALL

It all began in the 1930's with a fellow named T. Bill Duggan when he started a medical fund for injured players and a fund for baseball equipment. Through his encouragement and inspiration more than one hundred boys ranging in age from eight to thirteen became involved in organized baseball. Duggan's unselfish activity attracted the involvement of over five hundred businessmen who energized a new interest in sandlot baseball. Cleveland is said to be the first city to sponsor youth baseball, complete with equipment and uniforms.

The amateurs too, were having their day with Duggan's organization of the Cleveland Baseball Federation. The city's interest was evident when thousands of rooters cheered the local teams at Brookside Park Bowl, competing in national championships. Cleveland has longed claimed to be the "Sandlot Capitol of the World".

Also in the late 1930's I.S. "Nig" Rose, active in the baseball federation and the City's Recreational Department, formed the Municipal Softball Association. Softball adopted baseball guidelines and streamlined the rules to make it more exciting for spectators and players.

Cleveland sandlot baseball gave many youngsters in the 1940's and 50's an opportunity to develop and compete at various levels. Class "F" provided equipment, tee shirts, and hats for the teams. From there participants could move up to classes D, C, B, and A.

A class "D" team sponsored by A. Ceo's Red Circle Lanes was managed by Tiny Heitz and coached by Al Brandenburg. They won the city championship and then went on to compete in the National Amateur Baseball Federation Jr. Championship in Altoona Pennsylvania. They finished third.

Class "A" baseball had some of the most competitive games that ever took place at Edgewater Park and Brookside Park on any given Sunday or weekday evening. Many of the outstanding teams such as Rosenblums, Radiarts, Wenham Truckers, Knapp Wines, Factory Furniture and others would provide great entertainment for the hardball fans. Cleveland is very proud of names like Rich Rollins, Howard Krause, Dick Ciacchi, Jerry Patrick, and Frank Petruno. These greats either played professional baseball or were aspiring for an opportunity to someday make it to the big leagues.

Today baseball is more organized and structured with newer and more improved playing facilities. Years ago, young boys sought out fields where they could place their makeshift bases. In the "Angle" area many pick-up games and regular scheduled practices took place at the Cleveland Filtration Plant located at 45th Street and Lakeshore Drive. It was here where they find-tuned their skills among the many manhole covers scattered about the grassy outfield. St. Malachi's CYO practices were also held at the Filtration Plant. A vacant area near St. Malachi's between West 28th Street and Washington Avenue was also a popular spot for daily pick-up games.

Because of the excellent programs, many youngsters were given an opportunity to compete against the best talent in the city and in some instances, at national level tournaments. Thanks to all those who made a sincere contribution of their time in developing the youth of Cleveland.

– By Garry Roggenburk

CSU ARCHIVES – THE CLEVELAND PRESS\COLLECTION

WHAT
WE DID
FOR FUN . . .

Remember when...

the Cleveland Press headlines read "Cleveland Indians Win the American League Pennant!" How we loved baseball!

...times spent watching games down at Edgewater and at Brookside Park.

...Edgewater Park and family outings at its large picnic area. Maybe you spent a Saturday fishing off the rocks. You could change in the bath houses before going swimming, too.

...the Rollercade in full roll, and Halloran Park and Thrush Field where little league learned the sport.

Remember...

...all the Mom and Pop stores where you'd cash in pop bottles for a popsicle? or going to the corner drugstore to get a nickel cherry coke at the soda fountain? Or cutting through the alley to get over to your friend's house, so you could play hoola-hoop or hop-scotch?

...the thousands of side streets in the area were perfect playgrounds.

...piecing bike parts together so you could have "wheels?"

... playing one of the many street games like Release the Dungeon, Spud, Hide and Go Seek, Red Rover, or just playing stickball in the alleys?

...walking to the movies on a Saturday afternoon? You could spend a dime and watch the double feature cartoons all day. The movie theaters were all over the place--Madison, Variety, Little Lorain, Stork, Capital, Lyric,

DRAWIINGS: COLLEEN CORRIGAN

20

RUBBISH PICKIN'

Lyceum, and the Hipp! Remember "free dish" nights?

Did you ever have a big night at the Aragon? Or maybe you got to go on a day trip to Puritas Springs.

...standing in the line at West Tech, to get the new-found polio vaccine. Mr. Tuck, the principal at West Tech, kept traffic moving orderly between classes with his strict policies, too.

Remember when...

Cleveland had its own hockey team, the Barons. Maybe you went down to the Arena to see them play.

...an evening spent at home listening to the radio was a popular way to pass time

...evenings were spent listening to Amos & Andy, Burns and Allen, Inner Sanctum, Jack Benny and others on the radio

...black and white T.V. came on the scene and you could watch I Remember Mama; Red Skelton Show; Kukla, Fran and Ollie; the Ed Sullivan Show; Milton Berle; the Little Rascals and the Gene Carroll Show on the tube.

...pizza parlors came to Cleveland?

Wasn't it fun?

– Patricia Ehlen .Milenius

The rationing and conservation efforts of World War II, close on the heels of the hunger and scrimping of the Depression years, made everyone in the country somewhat thrifty. In Cleveland, we had two different waste collections — one was garbage day, for burnables; the other was rubbish day, for non-burnables. These were sorted for all kinds of recycling. Cans even had to be flattened to save space.

Stretched across the Near West Side were numerous routes for rubbish pick-up. Rubbish would be lined up on tree lawns, street after street. Perhaps the conservation conditioning made the people do it. But you know the saying: "One person's rubbish is another's treasure."

So, often you'd see people rubbish picking. Maybe they'd find bike parts, or old boots, or old toasters or irons that might be able to be fixed or used for parts. Maybe there would be hub caps, or parts of fencing, an old watering can, or hose, or a lantern. Sometimes people could even sell some stuff to someone else and make some money.

Rubbish picking had its pluses: it helped lessen the load for the rubbish men; it helped someone in need; it helped promote some potential creativity; and it helped in recycling. There may be even more pluses.

And then there probably were some negatives — like, messing up a neatly-packed box of rubbish; accumulating more junk in your garage that eventually had to be put out in your own rubbish bin; getting dirty and smelly; having neighbors look at you strangely.

But then, that's the way it was. And maybe the Near West Side wasn't too much different than other neighborhoods when it came to rubbish.

– H.K.G.

THE GORDON NEIGHBORHOOD

Norman Thorne was born in 1922 and lived next to Gordon School on W. 68th. His father was killed in an accident when Norman was eight. He remembers that his sisters and brothers had to pitch in to help Mom with money. He would shovel sidewalks. When he gave his Mom money, she always gave him back 25 cents for the movies.

Summertime at Gordon playground was great. There was kite flying, making leather crafts, marble tournaments and the baseball diamond. George, the cop, served as a crossing guard by Gordon School. Norman also went to Gordon Square Roller Rink — it had a huge wood floor and the Capital Theater was just upstairs. Movies were 5 cents each and Saturday matinee was at 1:00 p.m. The westerns were best, especially those with Tom Mix, or adventures, with Buck Rogers. Best of all was the 5 cent popcorn.

Back then, schools had paper drives. Whichever room did the best got an ice cream treat. Kids would go house to house collecting with a wagon.

The best place for ice cream was Thompson's Corner, Franklin and W. 58th, because they had 28 flavors. A double dip was 5 cents. As a kid, Norman liked banana, but they had root beer, black raspberry, pistachio, tutti-frutti and so much more.

Halloween was special back then. Beggar's (Bum's) Night (Oct. 30th) was for trick or treating. His grandmother would bake fresh donuts for kids. On that night you'd do mischievous things, like stick a straight pin in the doorbell so it would keep ringing. Most kids stayed home or went to a friends for a Halloween party on the 31st — you dunked for apples, pinned the tail on the donkey, and got goodies for both nights!

Sometimes he and some friends would play "knights" with wooden shields and stick swords. Once a friend took the new trash can lid and played. The boy's Dad yelled at him so loud the entire street heard.

About 16 kids played together. They used to attend the Y.M.C.A. and were given free tickets to the Indians games at League Park. The kids would take a streetcar to Lexington Avenue and E. 79th. In 1932, the Indians started playing weekends at the Stadium. Norman saw Babe Ruth and Lou Gehrig there. About 30,000 usually attended these games, and the most remarkable thing to him about the park was it had one "monster" wall, which made it tough for home runs.

A couple of the jobs he got as an older child and teenager stick in his mind —working as a caddy at Metroparks during the summer and as a pin setter at the bowling alley on W. 25th and Franklin. He got 25 cents a lane and took care of two lanes. He sold Cleveland Press papers for 3 cents each. He got 1 1/2 cents from each.

That's how things were back then.
– Rebecca Toney

WINTER FUN

To a kid in the 40's and 50's, winter outdoor fun meant the usual snowball fights, snowman building, finding fields where you could ice skate, slicking down an alley or small side street on which to play "hockey", or finding (or making) the best hill you could to go sled riding.

People in and around the Near West Side had limited numbers of cars, so traffic wasn't a big problem for outdoor play. In fact, a car here and there provided a certain kind of game for some of the more daring kids in the neighborhood — mostly boys. They could always hear a car coming because of the chains people used to put over their wheels. These chains pre-dated snow tires and were essential for getting through snowy or icy roads and hills, especially for stick-shift autos.

So, the "game" went like this: you'd hear a car coming, hide behind a snow drift, or pole, or something, until after the car slowly made its way past you. Just past you. Then you'd crouch down and hang onto the car's rear bumper and get pulled along the icy road for a free ride. We all wore those rubber boots over our shoes, and they were great for sliding, especially if the soles were worn smooth. It was fun, until parents saw us and screamed at us about how we could slip under the car and get killed.

Whatever game we'd play, we'd have to do it on the first couple of days after a fresh snow. You see, once the City Street Department got to the side streets with their cinders, the play areas were ruined. The cinders were brown, black and sooty; they were great for giving traction to cars, but awful to look at and terrible for winter games.

Cinders were discontinued sometime in the early 50's; it was discovered they gunked-up the sewer lines. Rock salt, however, soon replaced the cinders to cut our fun; it melted the snow!
– H.K.G.

ROLLERCADE

Of all the memories that make me smile, my days at the Rollercade were the best. Rollercade! Now that was a skating rink. It was located at 6800 Denison. It was huge! I went on Thursday nights because it was less crowded. Sometimes I went on Saturday nights or Sunday afternoon.

I went with a girlfriend, or even by myself. I loved to skate! I'd be there when it opened at 7:30 a.m. I remember thinking how big it was, when I first skated there.

If you didn't have skates, you could rent them. I'd skate in the big rink; there was a circle in the middle for the real good skaters. I learned the Circle Waltz and the Collegiate, which were easy, but I didn't learn any special dances, like the Tango.

The Rollercade was an equestrian style rink, so that's why it was so big. It had spectator seats on the right, which could have held a thousand people. Above the entrance, there was also a rink for the skaters who were members. And, of course, there was a refreshment stand with hot dogs, hamburgers, drinks, etc., and a clothes check, which was free.

They had a "robbers waltz" which I liked best, because I was sure to have a partner for at least one dance.

I wished Jack Dalton would have made his successors keep the rink, but they sold it for a supermarket, which also closed down. I wish they would turn it into a rink again.

I also skated at the Puritas Rink, although it was about half of the size of the Rollercade. But they had a great organist, named Ken Domby. That whole Park is gone, so the last time I went skating, was at Skateland on West 130th and Brookpark. I saw quite a few familiar faces, but I doubt if I'll go skating again. Getting too old!

— *Helen DiBin*

CSU ARCHIVES – THE CLEVELAND PRESS COLLECTION

CSU ARCHIVES – THE CLEVELAND PRESS COLLECTION

EARLY NINETEENTH CENTURY IMMIGRANTS' CONTRIBUTION TO THE CITY OF CLEVELAND

Many immigrants from Ireland, Germany, Czechoslovakia, and Hungary came to the U.S.A. between 1900 and 1920 to seek a better life. Most settled on the west bank of the Cuyahoga River in Cleveland. They were skilled in many trades, from farming to building. The men worked long hours in steel mills until they earned enough capital to open small businesses. Others bought land for farming and brought their fruits and vegetables to sell at the West Side Market.

Catholicism was a principal religion of these early settlers. Eventually, each nationality erected a Catholic Church in their neighborhood which became the focal point of worship and recreation. The Irish built St. Patrick's and St. Malachi's; the Germans, St. Mary's (which is now a chapel at St. Ignatius High School); the Slovaks, St. Wendelin's; and the Hungarians, St. Emeric's. Homes were erected around these churches. Catholic schools became their next project. Cleveland rapidly became a densely populated city.

Lorain Avenue was a beehive of activity. It resembled Fifth Avenue in New York City. The street was lined with commercial businesses of every kind. People were friendly, happy, and hopeful. Language was no barrier.

The West Side Community House on Bridge Avenue offered many recreational advantages to children after school and during summer vacation such as art, craft, candy making, etc., as did the Carnegie Branch Library, which scheduled story hours and books for every age group.

This was a good time to have lived and witnessed the growth of our city to the present.

– Mary Hillman

A MAN TO REMEMBER

CSU ARCHIVES – THE CLEVELAND PRESS COLLECTION

Many people have played important roles in the development of the West Side of Cleveland. One gentleman stands out among them. Mr. Jacob B. Perkins (1854-1936) lived on a knoll above the beaches of Lake Erie. As detailed in the Encyclopedia of Cleveland History (Van Tassel & Grabowski, 1987), in 1885, he built his family home of "Twin Elms" there. Below, in his meadow and beach area, was his personal race track of about 50 acres; quite a treat for an avid horse lover!

His estate was comprised of all the land north of the New York Central tracks to Lake Erie, east of what is now West 105th, and west of West 76th Street. Besides Twin Elms, Jacob Perkins had six buildings on his property, one of which was a carriage house. Many well-known Cleveland individuals lived along side him, including Mark and Leonard Hanna. These vast estates were in lengthy walking distance and much of the travel, or visiting, in the late 1800's was done by horseback. On any given day, you could see those neighbors riding along Lake Avenue, an unpaved cinder road at the time.

In 1894, thanks to his foresight and concern for others, Jacob Perkins gave a portion of his vast land, including his meadow and race track area to the city of Cleveland to be used as a park and recreation area. This gift was wonderful, but he didn't stop there.

As a Cleveland industrialist, he co-owned Hill Clutch Company, and could be seen in the late 1800's – early 1900's riding his horse to work at West 65th Street. Being a businessman, he understood that a strong neighborhood was important. So he helped with the construction of row houses on property from West 58th to West 65th and sold them on land contract/mortgage to the large influx of Irish and Italian immigrants, many of whom were employed at his plant. This allowed them a home and security.

When the Perkins Family decided to move from the area in 1913, he had his carriage house transported on a barge across Lake Erie to his new home in Mentor. His reason for this move came when requests were made from so many to sub-divide the land to allow others to enjoy the clean air, water and better transportation on the West Side.

Until his death in 1936, Jacob Perkins worked at his company, later called Hill Acme, but people will long remember him for the gift of a beach...for today, that beach is called Edgewater Park, formerly fondly called Perkin's Beach. The park was the site for ballroom dancing in the early 1900's, one of the first bath houses in Cleveland, and has also been the site for many memorable events—from a German Day in 1933 to the Festival of Freedom which is held yearly on July 4th with massive fireworks displays. Jacob Perkin's vision and caring for the Cleveland area, especially for the Near West Side, has brought a tremendous amount of joy and pleasure to so many. We salute his memory!

– Rebecca Toney

CSU ARCHIVES – THE CLEVELAND PRESS COLLECTION

29

EARLY 1900's

I'll soon be 85. I keep hearing "tell us when you were little grandma" from my greatgrands. They are fascinated by the tales of horse and wagon delivery of baked goods, the milkman who put the milk right into the ice box in the summer. In the winter it was left on the porch and, ah, the joy of finding it with a "high hat" of frozen cream! A farmer brought a buggy filled with fresh vegetables, homemade butter, a crate of live chickens, and fresh eggs.

How about the lamplighter with his small sort of step stool on his shoulder as he went from lamppost to lamppost lighting the gas street lights. He was always followed by children and knew us all by name. We were allowed to follow him from the lamp at our house to the next lamp.

I lived at 3161 W. 94th St and went to St. Ignatius School at W. Blvd. and Lorain. If you lived too far to go home for lunch, you carried a bag lunch and ate at your desk; the school didn't have a cafeteria. On Fridays the whole school smelled of egg sandwiches! I went to West Tech High. We had a Maypole & I was chosen one of the dancers to dance and weave ribbons around the pole. "Grandma, you danced around a pole?!" I ended up at Lakewood High when my family built a house on Arthur Ave.

My father owned a Tailoring and Mini Furnishing store on Lorain at 93rd St. and had two telephones as we did at home - Ohio Bell and Cuyahoga. There was a small picture show on the next street — 93rd St just off Lorain, and it cost one nickel. I went with my brother who was two years older. He hated taking his little sister, and one Sunday afternoon watching a cowboy show and racing train, my brother told me to go out the side door and tell the cowboys that the train was coming. I did as he told me, only to find myself outside in the bright sunlight of a quiet Sunday afternoon, lost in the alley behind the movie house. Fortunately a neighbor came by and recognized me: a phone call later, my father came to get me and gave my brother Holy H—l for pulling such a stunt on me.

I remember going to the Lorain Library on Saturday mornings with my brother for a story hour. He would take me in and seat me; then he would go off with his friends. That was fine until I received an award for perfect attendance and my mother protested because he didn't get one — then the truth came out.

We had two horses, Dolly and Nellie and a surrey (with the fringe on top) and a fancy rig for Sundays. A big red sleigh which both horses would pull for transportation was used in the winter. Across the street from our house on W. 94th we owned some land and built a big barn to house the horses.

– *Hildegarde Gorman*

"PAPER REX" MAN

CSU ARCHIVES – THE CLEVELAND PRESS COLLECTION

He was probably one of the last remnants of the horse and buggy history of Cleveland. Certainly on the Near West Side, he was the last to drive a buckboard drawn by a strong workhorse.

Anyone growing up on the West Side during the first half of the 20th century can probably remember the sounds—the buckboard's metal wheels rolling over the neighborhood's red brick streets, the clopping of the big old horse's hoofs, and most clearly, that certain way of calling out: "pa-a-per ray-cks". We all thought the paper-rags man yelled "paper-rex", and yet all knew that he was the junk man who'd pay you for newspapers, rags, and certain items that he knew how to recycle or sell to salvage companies.

It was a real wonder to know about the paper rags man. He rarely smiled, this entrepreneur. He was on the short side, dressed in overalls, and always wore one of those snap-brimmed hats. He had a scarf to catch the sweat he'd work up from spending the days riding under the summer sun. He drove right down the middle of the small side streets, stopping his rig if someone came out of their house to flag him down. While the adults haggled over business, if the ragman wanted to "buy" an item or not that day, the kids gathered around the horse, to pet him. Horses were pretty big stuff to city kids, and this horse was pretty friendly. Sometimes you might even sneak him a carrot or sugar cube, but generally, the driver didn't have much time for extra talk.

Before long, the paper-rags man was climbing back up on his seat, adjusting any junk that needed it in the buckboard, and clicking to his horse to "get-yup". Off he went, yelling out "paper-rex" again.

And, as anyone might imagine, sometimes the old horse had left a "calling card" behind him on the street—a real amazement to the kids!

But that's the way it was—and we all wondered what happened when this solitary man in his legendary trade appeared no longer on our streets.
– H.K.G.

WEST SIDE MEMORIES

My memories of life on the Near West Side, during the Great Depression in the 1930's, are a mixture of happy days and a slow-paced life, coupled with memories of a time of want.

At first, we lived on Lawn Avenue. I attended Lawn Elementary School. Some of my classmates came from the new Lakeview Terrace "family units." We envied those kids because they had central heating in their austere but comfortable apartments. We then moved to the corner of Madison and West 93rd Street, where I attended London Elementary School. One of my teachers was Margaret Middleton, who is still active at the West Side Community House.

This house seemed like it was 100 years old, at that time. We had a coal stove in the living room for heat and a coal stove in the kitchen. The one in the kitchen was for heat, cooking, toasting bread and drying clothes. In those days, we never stopped to think that these stoves could be safety hazards; we were glad just to keep warm.

We spent summer hours at Perkins Beach (at Edgewater) using the same bathhouse that stands today. People with money stopped for hamburgers at Poskey's – at the corner of Lake and Edgewater Drive, later called Don's Lighthouse and today known as Bistro 89.

In the late 30's, my sister went to West Technical High School, which had 5,000 students and was reported to be the largest high school in Ohio. The principal, Mr. C. C. Tuck, had his after school "track team" for anyone who didn't follow the rules - and compared to today, those were really very simple rules. They just expected you to behave. About that time, West Tech won the city football championship, and I remember the victory celebration getting out of hand.

We attended Sunday School at the Madison Avenue Baptist Church, which was just down the street. My baptism was a complete immersion in a pool of water on the sanctuary stage.

Some of the sad memories include my father being out of work and me not being able to take trumpet lessons. The lessons were $1.00 a week and you ended up owning the trumpet.

I guess the important thing was we really didn't know how poor we were, because everyone we knew was in the same boat. Most families did not look for outside help, but felt it was their responsibility to figure things out for themselves.

Because of my Depression background, I still have trouble getting rid of tangible things. In the Depression, we didn't throw anything away. Today I do share clothes, food and other items with the many West Siders who need help. I'm ever thankful for being able to have things in my adult life that we didn't have when I was young.

Was life better then or now? Each person must answer that question themselves.

— *George M. Keith*

32

JAMES
FORD
RHODES

James Ford Rhodes was a businessman, author and historian, born on May 1, 1848 at Franklin Circle in the Near West Side of Cleveland. James' father was Daniel Pomeroy Rhodes, a Cleveland industrialist in the coal-mining trade. His mother, Sophia Lord Russell Rhodes, was the granddaughter of Josiah Barber, co-founder and first mayor of Ohio City.

According to the Encyclopedia of Cleveland History (Van Tassel and Grabowski, 1987) James Ford Rhodes graduated from West High School in 1865. He later went on to college and traveled abroad where he studied his first love, history, and French literature. Due to his father's interests in coal-mining, he decided to study iron metallurgy. He visited iron and steel mills in Europe and the United States. In 1870, he came back to Cleveland and joined his father's firm. In 1872, he married Ann Card and they had a son, Daniel Pomeroy, in 1876.

In 1874, he and several partners, including his brother, Robert, brother-in-law Marcus A. Hanna, Charles Bolton, Arnold Saunders and George H. Warmington began a mining company.

In 1881, Rhodes began to write successful trade circulars. In 1884, he decided that he was financially secure enough to retire from his business. He began a 43 year career of studying and writing history. He published, lectured, and although he had not completed college, received numerous honors and honorary degrees. In 1898-99, he was president of the American Historical Association.

James Ford Rhodes died in Massachusetts in 1927. His ashes were brought back to Cleveland and are buried at Riverside Cemetery. But his memory lives on. In 1932, a new high school at 5100 Biddulph Avenue was named James Ford Rhodes High School in dedication to his love for history and his devotion to education.

He was also honored among nationally and internationally acclaimed Clevelanders when, in 1971, the City established its Hall of Fame and included James Ford Rhodes.

– Rebecca Toney

WEST SIDE COMMUNITY HOUSE

The West Side Community House holds a very special place in the minds and hearts of people who grew up in the Near West Side. Whether it was because they went there as newcomers to Cleveland to get help, went there for entertainment like dances or roller skating on the wood floors in the basement, attended the day camps, took classes there, or just played on their playground...whatever... the Community House (or more fondly, "C" House) has been there for a long time to provide activities for neighborhood people.

The Community House Centennial Report (1890-1990) tells us of their beginning through the Methodist Episcopal Deaconess Home (organized through the Women's Home Missionary Society). Their purpose was to help settle many new immigrants (mostly German and Irish) who left their homeland to enter their new community in Cleveland. Most were living in poverty due to economic hard times. The Home helped with food, clothing, shelter, language, etc.

The Homes began on the east side, around 1890, then extended downtown. In 1900, a deaconess with Franklin Avenue Church realized that a poverty area existed around the church. There were no social services available to immigrants. By 1904, the Methodist Episcopal Deaconess Home opened to help West Siders at 78 Hicks St. (now W. 28th St.). There was a nursery, a kindergarten, a dispensary for women and children, classes in kitchen and industrial skills, clubs for boys and girls, and meetings for adults. The demand for services grew and, in 1905, the Home was moved to 2045 W. 25th Street.

In 1908, the property at West 30th and Bridge was purchased. There were three houses on the land — one for the resident workers, one for the nursery and the third for kindergarten, club work and storage.

In 1914, the name offically became Deaconess Community House. At that time, the Community House began English classes and an employment department (later taken over by Goodwill Industries) to help women find jobs. Many men were out of work. Women had to help to survive.

By 1922, a new building was built on the 30th and Bridge address, costing $240,000. It had 91 rooms, including space for 40 workers to live. Services were increased, to include holding Americanization classes.

During the 1940s, a shift in population began, from European immigrant to lower income Appalachians and Puerto Rican immigrants.

In 1944, the charter of the Home was changed to make the Community House a non-sectarian, professional and community-oriented facility. At that time, professional workers were hired to replace the deaconesses working there.

In 1960, a Board of Managers took over ownership and operation of the West Side Community House.

Today, "C" House continues to help residents of the West Side through elderly services, youth services, daycare, evening "hot meals" and more. The Community House has been an endearing friend to thousands of families for over 100 years.

– Rebecca Toney

DAY
CARE
BABY

I was a West Side Community House baby from the age of one and a half. I was cared for by Methodist laywomen, called deaconesses, who lived in the large wooden residence next door to Community House. My mother told me later that one of them, Merle Naylor, kept me in her room every evening after the Community House Nursery closed, until my mother could get there from work. The year was 1929.

My own memories of Miss Naylor begin about age three, when I remember her steathily taking me from the crib at naptime (I had been wailing well) and taking me out to the sandbox. It is impossible to describe how much her attention meant in my life, and, I'm sure, in the lives of the others. Pictures she took of me, of others, of the building, are my treasured possessions.

Sometime in 1932, I went from the Nursery side of Community House (to the left of the stairway) to the Big Kid side (to the right of the stairway). For the next few years:

I entered through the wide metal doors off Bridge Avenue in the early morning, always sleepy. I walked up the wide front stairs, smelling the Community House smell, and feeling at home. I arrived at the entrance of a brightly lit room, and a woman, seated at a small table, handed me a tablespoonful of cod liver oil. I swallowed it quickly and grabbed the small orange juice chaser. The worst part of the day was over.

I walked past the room with a fireplace and into a small room toward the back where our boxes were. The whole wall was boxes, each one with a name on it, and each one holding the blanket that person would use for naptime. There I put my hat and mittens, and, on the opposite wall, hung my coat. I then returned to the room with the fireplace and went to one of the long tables where the kids my age were making puzzles and other put-together type games.

A short while later, we four-years old walked from Community House to Kentucky Elementary for kindergarten. Since we were younger than the neighborhood children who went to kindergarten, the public school must have made a special arrangement for the Community House children.

Kindergarten was a world of creativity: paints, crayons, every kind of paper, from tissue to cardboard, paste and scissors. We made child-size cardboard houses that we could walk into, and painted windows, shutters, doors and flowers on the outside walls, and curtains, pictures and people on the inside walls. I loved every minute.

When we children returned to the Community House after our morning kindergarten, dinner was ready. My favorite food of all time is the cracked wheat bread they baked every day there. The aroma thickened the air around us and drew us to the table, ravenous.

You've heard of Euclid Beach ice cream, but it cannot be compared to Community House ice cream. This custardy vanilla ice cream had a taste to die for. The rumor always began as we got up from our naps. Ordinarily, this would be playground time, but none of us bothered with that now. We assembled on the back porch and sat along the stone ledges, waiting. The boys did not fight with the girls, the boys did not push each other off the ledges. We all just waited. It was always worth the wait.

The Community House world was entirely separate from my life with my mother. After one of our many moves to the East Side, I could pretty much pick up where I left off at Community House, whereas my other life always involved a different neighborhood and another school.

In 1936, we were living on the East Side and mother obtained a job at Fries & Schuele on West 25th Street. In the middle of the winter and in the middle of the school year, we moved again, back to what was to me the prime West Side location: Mrs. Budenborg's house on the corner of Bridge and West 30th Street. From the top floor where we lived, I could look across Bridge Ave. at all the comings and goings at Community House, and then across West 30th St. to all the comings and goings at Heckman's Candy Store. It's a tossup which of these two landmarks drew the most people in a day.

In 1937, I finished fourth grade at St. Mary's; returned to Sunday School at Community House and was Miss America in their Fourth of July Pageant at the Methodist Church (in my let-down First Communion dress); and spent two weeks at the Epworth Fresh Air Camp.

The top floor of Mrs. Budenborg's house was stifling and airless that summer. Long into the night, I sat on my bed with my face against the screen, hoping for a breeze. It was then I discovered that the corner in front of Heckman's was just as interesting in the middle of the night as it was during the day. More so.

On any given night there were as many as ten or twelve boys gathered there, hatching their plots, smoking their secret cigarettes. Most of the plots were a mystery to me - I could never catch enough of the dialogue. But one plot was quite plain, since it was acted out in front of me.

Two or three boys would leave the group and saunter casually up West 30th toward St. Mary's. A short time later, distantly, I would hear the sound of shattering glass. Then, suddenly, the same boys would run back down West 30th to the group on the corner, where, still panting, they arranged themselves in bored po-sitions against the walls of Heckman's just in time to see the fire engine race around the corner and scream up to St. Mary's.

Later, a couple of the firemen might stop by the corner to talk to the boys still there. The boys, of course, had seen nothing.

We moved from the neighborhood in September of 1938, one day before I started sixth grade. My mother had bought a bungalow off West 130th street, our permanent home. Three years later, I returned daily by bus and streetcar to attend St. Stephen's High School, from which I graduated in 1945. Another four years after that, I returned to St. Stephen's to teach the fourth grade.

In 1950, newly married, my husband and I rented the rear house at 1833 West 54th St., and lived there until the tornado of 1953, when a hundred foot tree in our living room made the house uninhabitable.

Perhaps as devastating is the fact that while we lived there in the summer of 1952, there were eight cases of polio on West 54th, the highest incidence in a neighborhood in the city. When I needed groceries, I left my daughter at home alone in her playpen, rather than take her with me to Fisher's at the corner of Bridge and 54th. The doctor had assured me that polio was not contagious, but I could not take the chance that he might be wrong.

In 1982 I returned to the West Side Community House as a volunteer in its Evening Meals Program, and stayed until September of 1990.

—Joan Dunn Gill

PIZZA,
POTATO CHIPS,
ICE CREAM –
BACK WHEN

The early 50's saw pizza arrive on the Cleveland scene. It was a fad that grew increasingly more popular until it became a part of Americana. Pizza is everywhere - big cities and small towns, it's baked, topped and prepared in countless combinations. On West 65th and Lorain, "Joe Peeps Never Sleeps" was a landmark for many years. It was a small storefront with living quarters in the rear, as it was a family operation. The first pizza they sold was purchased from Fiocca's, which then and now is an Italian bakery on West 69th, just north of Detroit. It consisted of a rather thick crust, a light sauce and a sprinkling of spaghetti-style cheese. Eventually, they began making the type of pizza we are all familiar with, but I've been told that their original is the real Italian pizza. A few other places I remember from the early 50's include Peppi's on 98th and Denison (still there), Francesca's on West 105th, Miranda's in Parma, and CiCi's on West 54th and Lorain, which was a hang-out for me and many of my friends. The young of today go to malls to socialize, but the pizza parlor, with its booths and juke box, was all we needed.

The predecessors of the Dairy Queens and Baskin Robbins were neighborhood ice cream parlors. In the 40's, no vendors drove down the streets selling ice cream, and many people did not have refrigerators with freezers. We had ice boxes. A hot summer night wasn't complete without a walk to Thompkins Corner at West 44th and Lorain, or Kantor's on West 57th and Bridge, for a double dipper. Of the two, Thomp-kins Corner was my favorite, as it had as many as 30 flavors to choose from. It was a big decision whether blackberry ripple or orange-pineapple would be the choice for that evening. Lorain Avenue had many people walking to and from the ice cream parlor, so it was a good time for a lot of socializing.

I grew up on West 47th, on the north side of Lorain Avenue, just a few houses from the Num Num potato chip factory, a small business that employed many of my neighbors. In the warm months, the opaque windows would be open and we could see the chips travelling along conveyor belts and being bagged. They closed in the late 40's or early 50's, and for me and other neighborhood kids, we lost a source of free goodies. Outdated (usually stale) chips were dumped into an open truck and, when no one was looking, we helped ourselves to the broken and "not so fresh" treats. That was as close as I came to being a juvenile delinquent.

I still love pizza, ice cream and potato chips, and it would sure be nice to stroll Lorain Avenue and see the neon signs beckoning to me again. Time changes many things, but memories only get better!

— *Carol Sabo*

THE
CORNER
STORE

At the corner of W. 82nd and Denison stood a store named George's, owned by a white haired Greek man named, what else, Mr. George. Mr. George, as I remember, was a little crotchety old man who did not like me. He preferred the kids who did not give him a hard time. I can remember going into his store and sitting at the soda fountain, on a green stool that I could do a full 360 degree turn upon. One time, I can remember doing so many turns that the stool fell off and Mr. George threw me out, threatening to call my father and the police, not necessarily in that order. I can also remember going to that same soda fountain and getting a two scoop chocolate ice cream soda for twenty five cents, or, for thirty cents, a vanilla milkshake that was so cold it gave you a headache if you drank it too fast. I could also get a long neck Pepsi and two pretzel sticks for ten cents. Upon returning my empty bottle for its two cent deposit, I would then promptly spend it on Mr. George's display of excellent penny candy.

The thing I remember the most was that Mr. George made all of his candy by hand, different candies on a daily basis. I remember the showcase being about twelve feet long and taller than I could see over. Starting on the left of the showcase were all the chocolate covered creams, piled up three and four layers high. You knew they were made by hand because there was always some chocolate that had dripped down on the paper that separated the rows. All of the creams were the size of walnuts, orange, lemon, cherry, lime, strawberry, maple, chocolate, and vanilla, covered in light or dark chocolate. Next to the creams were the chocolate covered cherries. I cannot describe them because there are no words in my vocabulary to express how good they were. Then came the peanut clusters, chocolate covered walnuts and haystacks, then came Mr.

George's great contribution to mankind and the civilized world....the nutmallow. It was sheets of marshmallows covered in light or dark chocolate, generously sprinkled with walnuts. I am a better person for having eaten this nutmallow.

A very special time at Mr. George's was Easter, when the cases were filled with solid chocolate Easter bunnies and chicks, done in regular, dark or sometimes even green or pink chocolate. The pink chocolate was not one of Mr. George's best ideas. The bunnies and chicks were arranged in height and color, lined up like little soldiers in the showcase. The Easter display would grow in size in the showcase until about two weeks before Easter. Then the ranks of the chocolate bunnies would shrink daily. By Easter Sunday, they were all gone.

In the fall of 1961, I stopped in Mr. George's, to inform him that I had joined the army and would be leaving the next day. A large smile came to his face. He informed me that his prayers had been answered and, now that I was leaving, he was sure that there was a God in Heaven and he could live the rest of his life in peace.

When I came home the following summer, on leave before going overseas, I found out that Mr. George had retired and gone back to Greece. His son was running the store. I stopped in to get a milkshake and say hello. When I walked into the store, I was shocked to see the soda fountain was gone, replaced by a large standup cooler, loaded with Eskimo pies, Drumsticks, and frozen dinners. The candy case was half of its original size, filled with boxes of candy bars. I was devastated. Mr. George's son came out of the back room and asked me if I wanted something. I said "Yeah, but I'll have to go to Greece and find your father to get it... the best damn candy I ever ate".

—— *Bill Jenks*

ABBEY MARKET

The Abbey Market name still exists, but at a different location (across the street) and with a very different atmosphere. Today's market features lottery tickets and carry-out beverages, much different than the neighborhood store I remember.

One of my earliest memories of the store was being sent there by my grandmother, during the Second World War, with a ration stamp to purchase five pounds of sugar. I was probably about six or seven. When the owner told me that he had no sugar, I was naive enough to look around the store and point out to him that he had a lot of sugar — his special under-the-counter supply. I think this delighted him as well as the other customers in the store at the time, because he quickly took my money, placed the sugar in a bag, and ushered me out of the store. As the years passed, I can remember going there for candy, pop, and other things of importance to a young boy. During the years between elementary and high school, the store changed hands twice. I was employed by later owners to work behind the meat counter. I had had a short apprenticeship at Hartman's at the West Side Market and also worked for an uncle who owned Sunshine Foods, where I learned to cut meat with a fair amount of skill. I'm not sure why I left my uncle's store to go to work for Al and Mary; maybe it was because I no longer had to take a half hour bus ride to earn my spending and tuition money. Before the days of large food chains and refrigerated freezers, most people had to buy their meat almost on a daily basis. The large chains may have had a greater variety, but none of them offered the luxury of "putting it on the book"-- paying at the end of the month. Rarely did customers default in their payment. Although Al was a tank commander during the Second World War, it was usually Mary who confronted them with their obligation to pay their bills, so that she could pay hers.

Most of the customers were known by name. On weekends, several would call in their order. I would deliver them. I liked delivering because I got to drive the boss' Buick — sometimes not too gently. I can remember, the R B Cookie display, which held about sixteen five pound boxes of cookies. Each box was protected by a hinged glass cover, which fit over the front of the box. I am sure that every kid in the neighborhood had an opportunity to pick one of his favorite cookies out of the display. It may not have been very sanitary, but it turned out to be an excellent instructional aid in learning the magic word. Each winter a fifty-five gallon barrel of sauerkraut was delivered and placed in the large walk-in cooler. If necessary, Al would add just the right amount of salt to bring it up to the quality of previous years. The barrel usually lasted until spring. This too was dispensed in the same manner as were the cookies. During the winter Al would often make "Kochanina" (phonetic Slovak spelling), jelled pigs feet and bring plates of them to the store to sell. I never ate them then, but many foods become more attrac-

tive as one gets older. The season of Lent was a difficult time for business because at that time, Catholic adults ate meat only once a day. It was also a difficult time for Al, because he was allergic to cheese. We naturally ate lunch at the store, usually something simple, cooked on an electric hot plate. I can still vividly recall a Friday when Al walked into the cooler and spent what seemed to be a long period of time in there. When I opened the door, he quickly placed a half-eaten hot dog in his pocket and innocently walked out. Of course I exposed him immediately. Although he accused me of being crazy, the evidence was there when Mary made him empty his pockets.

Al died many years ago, but Mary and I are still good friends; we often laugh about that incident and many others. I fondly recall the many good times we shared. There was the salesman, from Anter Brothers I think, who could always tell you the exact number of days until Christmas; and of course the mailmen Joe and Tony, who often stopped in and chatted "for a few moments," when they weren't enjoying a practical joke such as pushing my car down the street; there was the customer who insisted that I cut off the part of the chicken which goes over the fence last before wrapping it for her; and others...

The money I made while working at Abbey Market helped pay my tuition in both high school and college, and was of considerable importance. The experience I gained working daily with the people of the community has been of lasting value.

—— Jim Chura

PENNY
CANDY

If you were a kid growing up in the 40's or 50's on the Near West Side, you were in pretty good shape if you could get your hands on a few pennies to buy candy. Pennies bought a fair amount of candy. A nickel bought a large candy bar. There was something quite magical about going to one of the corner stores and spending time peering through the glassed-in counter, trying to decide how to get the most candy for the few cents you had. Maybe you had found a few pop bottles to return for cash, or maybe you had made a few cents at a lemonade stand, or maybe you had an allowance, or maybe your Mom had a few cents at the bottom of her purse to give you, so you could go to the store with the other kids.

Corner stores often had their check-out counter double as the candy counter. You had to keep out of the way of regular adult customers. That usually worked in your favor, giving enough time to make good selections. Deciding what candy to buy, was tough. MaryJanes were 2 for a penny. Red hot chewy coins were 3 for a penny. There were frenchies, that white fluffy nougat, with colored jellies in them, for a penny. You could get 4 or 5 large malted milk balls for a penny. There were long paper strips of candy "pills" for a penny. Bullseyes were 2 for a penny. Root beer barrels were 2 or 3 for a penny. Jaw breakers were almost as big as walnuts, and one cost a penny. There was lik-m-aid, in little paper pouches, for a penny. There were 4 wax-bottles, each with a colored syrup in them, for a penny. There were those white sugar balls, with a hazelnut in the middle, for a penny. And there were waxed lips, teeth, moustaches, fingernails, each for a penny, to be worn until you decided to chew out all the sugar.

There were nonpareils, milk duds, black jacks, all 3 for a penny. There were watermelon-shaped coconut strips, and neopolitan strips for a penny. There were those banana-flavored soft circus peanuts, 3 for a penny. There were shoe string red licorice and black licorice pipes or whips, each for a penny. Double-bubble, Oh-Boy or Bazooka gum cost a penny, but the smaller bubble gums were 2 for a penny. There were chocolate covered vanilla creams that looked like little domes, peppermint patties, peanut butter logs, toasted coconut logs, each for a penny. There were those mini marshmallow ice cream cones for a penny; fireballs were 2 for a penny. Candy cigarettes cost a few pennies and candy lipstick was a penny; rock candy on a string was 1 cent and ribbon candy was a penny. Pretzel rods were 2 for a penny. If you felt lucky, you could put your penny in the gumball machine and hope that a striped gumball would come out on your crank. That would get you a free candy bar.

Kinds of candies seemed to vary by season and by store. But the "staples" would always return. For the few years that candy was important to you, as you grew up, those trips to the corner store became ingrained in your memory for life.
–H.K.G.

CSU ARCHIVES - THE CLEVELAND PRESS COLLECTION

43

CSU ARCHIVES – THE CLEVELAND PRESS COLLECTION

JOHN PATRICK "JOHNNY" KILBANE

John Patrick Kilbane was born in 1889 in the area of Cleveland's Near West Side called the "Angle"—W. 25th and Detroit. According to the Encyclopedia of Cleveland History (Van Tassel and Grabowski, 1987) his father was a steel worker who became blind when Johnny was only 6 years old. As soon as Johnny finished the 6th grade school requirement, he found a job as a switch tender for the New York P & O Railroad.

His dreams, however, were set on boxing. At 5'5" tall and 120 lbs. he was classed in the featherweight division. A famous boxer in the early 1900's was Jimmy Dunn. Kilbane met Dunn, who offered to train him to box. Kilbane said the first thing Dunn taught him was how "not to get hit."

Johnny's first fight was in December of 1907. He was paid $1.50 and carfare. In February 1912, Kilbane fought a title match against featherweight champ, Abe Attell, in California. He won a 20-round decision. He came home to Cleveland on St. Patrick's Day and was welcomed by over 100,000 Cevelanders as the new featherweight champion of the world.

During World War I, Kilbane worked as a physical trainer at Camp Sherman and Camp Gordon in Georgia. In September of 1921, he fought a match and won $60,000 for the fight. He didn't box again until 1923. He lost that fight, but received $75,000 for being a participant. He stopped fighting with a record of 142-4.

He then went to work for the Cleveland Public Schools, as a physical education instructor in 1934-35. In the 1940's he went on to politics, serving in the Ohio Senate and House of Representatives.

In 1951, he became a clerk of the Municipal Courts and remained there until his death in May of 1957. Called the "Most perfect fighting machine in the world" and Cleveland's "greatest champion," Kilbane left a mark of encouragement to other young boxers. St. Malachi Church, one block from where Johnny was born, has encouraged the sport and has had many Golden Glove awardees. All will remember the "Angle's" boxing hero.

– Rebecca Toney

RAIL TRANSPORTATION

Thoughts of passenger trains that once passed through the Near West Side area lead me, across the Cuyahoga River, to the Terminal Tower. In past years, the lower concourse (now part of The Avenue) was a maze of activity for rail passengers coming and going in many directions. Many celebrities and dignitaries arrived here by train. I remember the thrill I felt when President Eisenhower shook my hand and bid me good morning as he made his way up the ramp to the street level.

There is little of that era left. The only trains operating in and out of the tower are Regional Transit Authority (RTA). The tracks leading to the west were abandoned and subsequently torn up. Today, you might get a glimpse of the lone AMTRAK passenger train travelling thru the area to or from Chicago. Perhaps one day in the future, we will again be able to board a train and travel in almost any direction.

Also gone from the Tower are the many railroad offices and personnel which once occupied the vast majority of the office space.

The freight trains continue to operate thru the Near West Side area. Many of the spur lines leading to former companies, including the old stock yards, are no longer used. Times have changed. Business firms have moved or closed their doors, leaving many to poverty. The construction of highways, etc., took its toll on housing and businesses along the route. The railroads have survived through many years and much turmoil within the industry and will continue to operate. However, will the loss of industry and gainful employment ever be restored to this area?

– Maryanne Henderson

CSU ARCHIVES – THE CLEVELAND PRESS COLLECTION

ALLEYS

In today's world of highways and interstates, many people miss driving through neighborhoods. What today seems like a small neighborhood street, was really a major road during the first half of the 20th Century, when the automobile was a status means of transportation.

Major roads through the Near West Side were Lorain Avenue, Clark Avenue, Detroit Avenue; West 25th, West 65th, and 73rd. Denison capped off the southern end, while West Boulevard capped off the western side.

Roads were for cars and trucks, streetcars, buses, and bikes. Horses were still using them, here and there, into the 1950's. Whether they were the "big" streets like Lorain, or the thousands of side streets like Colgate or Cloud, their purpose was transportation.

But not the alleys. Dotted all around the Near West Side, alleys had a purpose and "beat," all their own. Small garages often opened onto them and a person could store cars in them. Many yards had gates that opened into the alley. People "cut through" the alleys when walking somewhere. Neighbors hob-nobbed in the alley catching up on what was happening in the neighborhood. And, of course, kids played in the alleys.

Alleys lent a kind of special social function to a neighborhood. Never really "beautiful" or maintained like the actual roads or streets, they still bore names of "court" or "lane," such as Fulton Court or Cyrano Lane.

As the 20th Century comes to a close,

there are still many alleys in the Near West Side. Some are gone to modern construction and/or neighborhood reconstruction. But alleys hold many secrets of a life slowly going by. They were playgrounds where kids hid from "cops and robbers" — they were "breezeways" between backyards where women could yell back and forth as they hung their laundry out to dry. They were even quiet paths where a man could walk alone and dream about the times to come.
– H.K.G.

STREET
SCENES

Time changes everything--hair styles, music, cars and even status symbols. The youth of today look to their feet. It's Nike, Converse, Puma, L.A. Gear, etc. that are the hot items in fashion. As a teenager on the lower west side in the mid 50's, shoes were a necessity, not a fashion statement. However, our $5.99 button-front Levi's were a must and, immediately after being purchased, they were soaked in bleach water for a few days to achieve that "been around" look. Back then, the big fad with me and my peers was tailor made drapes, and I don't mean the kind you hang on the windows.

They were dress slacks made at two local shops on West 25th Street – Liberty Tailors and Robb Tailors. For a mere $25.00 (big bucks then), you could pick out the material of your choice, and in about two weeks, you were ready to strut around the neighborhood. They were high-waisted with a pleated front, and pegged so tight at the ankle, you had to work to get them over your feet. For me, it took two Saturdays of working at the West Side Market to pay for them. But it was worth it when you walked into the Friday night dance at the "C" House (Community House) too cool for words, or went to the Lorain-Fulton Show (where I first met my husband in 1955).

The guys also wore drapes, and if you had more than four pair, you were to be envied. I had two pair, one black and one gray flannel, with high hopes of getting a powder-blue pair. I never did get them. Perhaps there were several new records that had to be bought, a trip to Euclid Beach, or maybe I passed on to another stage of growing up.

The many corners and storefronts of Lorain Avenue provided a place to stand on

those warm summer evenings. (My husband and I had our first date in front of the Hot Dog Inn on 41st and Lorain). Almost always we wore our Levi's, but when you wanted to make the big impression, it was time for drapes. Each evening, the streets were filled with hot rods, customs and beaters, along with kids like myself just hanging around.

Oh, to be 16 again!

P.S. The Puerto Rican community was small in the mid 50's, but they wore drapes quite often, and we would wonder how they got theirs pegged so tight. After a close look, we found they had them made with an inside seam zipper.
— *Carol Sabo*

BRIDGES

CSU ARCHIVES – THE CLEVELAND PRESS COLLECTION

East Side, West Side, all around the town. To get downtown one of various bridges must be crossed.

In the latter part of the 18th century, ferries were the means of transportation, when one wanted to venture east from the west side of the Cuyahoga. With the advent of cars and trucks, the use of the ferries became impractical or obsolete for traffic purposes.

In 1836, the 200 foot Columbus Street Bridge was erected incorporating sidewalks. This was supposed to be more substantial than the Center Street Bridge which had been built years earlier. When Cleveland and Ohio City were incorporated, Cleveland decided to destroy its part of the Center Street Bridge so that more business could take place by traffic using the Columbus Street Bridge, thereby bypassing Ohio City altogether. Outraged Ohio City residents caused a ruckus and, as a result, the Center Street

Bridge was retained. With the increase in traffic by 1854, it was necessary to build other bridges to handle the overload so the Main Street Bridge and the Seneca Street Bridge were constructed.

In 1932 the Lorain-Carnegie Bridge, later known as the Hope Memorial Bridge, was built. It was unique in structure because of its pylons with figures symbolizing the progress of transportation.

In 1993 close to a dozen bridges serving automobile traffic and trains remain spanning the Cuyahoga. Some are more historic than others but all play a role in the history of Cleveland's West Side.

So East Side, West Side, all around the town, tots sing ring around the rosie, but Cleveland's bridges don't fall down.

– V. A. *Kilbane*
(Information obtained from Encyclopedia of Cleveland, Van Tassed-Grabowski, 1987)

49

STOKYARDS

As a kid growing up on the West Side, I remember walking from school having to cross the railroad tracks to get to my house. Once in a while, I'd count the number of train cars while waiting and wonder if any hobos were hiding out in any of the cars. One vivid memory was the smell of the trains as they passed. You could see some pigs and cattle in a few of the cars and you immediately knew where the odor was coming from. These livestock were on their way to the stockyards to be slaughtered.

In Cleveland, the big stockyards were located on W. 65th St. It was often called the "Hotel de la Hoof" where the guests came in as animals and left as steaks, sausage or ham.

The seventh largest in the country in the 20's, Cleveland Union Stockyards consisted of over 60 acres of pens and bedding areas. A hotel and a bar were provided for the farmers who brought their livestock to market. The Cleveland Stockyards provided excellent quality stock at fair prices, attracting buyers from out of state as well as local merchants.

After the Second World War, the raising of livestock moved westward, so the industry declined in the Cleveland area. Representatives of packing houses went directly to the farmers, thereby eliminating the stockyards. Finally in 1968 the Cleveland Union Stockyards closed down for good.

Even though I don't cross the tracks to get home anymore, the memory of the smell of the livestock still lingers in my mind when I see a train pass by.

– V.A. Kilbane

Information in part from Encyclopedia of History of Cleveland, Van Tassel and Grabowski, 1987.

DRUGSTORES

Many scientific advancements have developed during the 20th century — some good, but maybe later discarded, others made better and better as the years went on. In the line of pharmaceuticals, the 1900's exploded.

Before I grew to understand the significance of how the business of pills, ointments, lotions and the like converged into environmental, economic and political questions, I just knew the corner drugstore. It had a very simple life: medical and social.

During the 40's and 50's, throughout the Near West Side and adjacent neighborhoods, drugstores were found aplenty. Like Liberty on Lorain and W.25th, or Funk's on Denison and W. 65th, or Ludwig's on W. 52nd and Storer, or Standard's, or Mac's and so on. They were often family-run and offered the aspirins, vaporubs, oils, liniments, syrups, prescriptions, hot water bottles, and whatever toiletries people found basic to everyday health. There were limited choices among each kind of syrup, or oil, but quite enough to enable you to pick out one and not go too crazy in trying to make a decision. All the bottle caps came off with a twist, pop or snap by even the youngest, or feeblest, of persons.

You could also buy other needs — small hardware things, soaps, thread, toilet paper, hair things, umbrellas, shoe polish and the like. A lot depended on the owner and what he thought he could sell to his customers. Different candies, ice cream novelties, pop, snacks, etc., were also often available.

Equally important to neighborhood people, the drugstores usually had soda fountains! There was nothing quite like stepping up to the long formica counter and sliding onto a slick stool to wait for someone to ask you your order. Often the "menu" of ice cream flavors, the list of sundaes, sodas, floats, shakes, malts and splits, was listed on the wall. It wasn't so much what you ordered that was so exciting (although I can't ever remember not relishing every drop of whatever I got), it was more being able to be with the few other people who were also at the fountain: The guy with the cup of coffee, the lady waiting for the milkshake machine to finish whirring her shake, the couple watching the waitress squirt piles of whipped cream on their banana splits.

Even more exciting to plenty of teens was the use the drugstore played in meeting that special someone to share a soda with. Some drugstores were even hangouts for teens, the fountains doing a brisk business between pops, ice cream, and burgers.

You made community in places like this. You knew people; they cared that you got just what you needed. And as the little bell chimed when the door opened or closed, customer and storekeeper had a warm greeting to each other.
– H.K.G.

BREWERIES

At the turn of the century, there were approximately 4,100 breweries around the country, with a high concentration in the Midwest. Like most large cities, Cleveland boasted some 30 breweries. Many of the breweries were neighborhood breweries, which were almost as common as neighborhood bars are today, each with its own distinct style and flavor.

In the early 1800s, most Cleveland breweries reflected the large English and Irish population in the city, specializing in ales, porters and stouts. The heavier ales were slowly replaced with lighter-bodied lagers. The tendency towards lagers was strong all over the country at that time and explains why most American beers today are lighter lagers.

Many of Cleveland's breweries, in her brewery glory days, were within a couple of blocks of Ohio City, most notably Gehring Brewery, on Brainard and Leisy's located on Vega Avenue, the Oppman Brewery on Columbus, the Whitlock Brewery on Canal and P.O.C. on Clark.

Prohibition devastated small, local breweries. In the 1930s, their numbers shrunk to a few hundred nation-wide. From there, the strongest survivors bought out many of the rest, reducing their numbers even more.

In 1936, only 11 breweries remained in Cleveland. Forest City Brewing Inc., located on Union Avenue, Standard Brewing Co., located on Train Avenue, Stroh Brewing Co. on E. 40th St. and P.O.C. on Clark were among them. Larger breweries continued to buy out the smaller ones. The larger operations also had the advantage of refrigerated trucks and sophisticated advertising campaigns. Hence, local breweries quickly became extinct.

In 1982, The Schmidt Brewery closed its doors, leaving Cleveland with no breweries to call its own. Fortunately, in the Fall of 1988, a new brewery opened in Cleveland. The Great Lakes Brewing Co., in the tradition of local breweries of the 1800s, opened as a micro-brewery, producing only 2,000 barrels of beer a year for thirsty Clevelanders. Like so many of its predecessors, it is located in Ohio City and pays homage to Cleveland breweries of yesteryear with old advertisements and memorabilia throughout the facility (which is also a restaurant or "brewpub").

With the Great Lakes Brewing Co.'s success, it seems Cleveland history has come full circle.

– *Mary Conway Sullivan*

SOME WEST SIDE "GOOD OLD DAYS" REFLECTIONS

According to Webster, the word "neighborhood" originally meant "friendly relations." And that's pretty much how three Greater Clevelanders remember the Near West Side world they grew up in, the West Side of the 20's and 30's.

Al, now of Westlake, and Lucille, of Rocky River, reminisce from some little distance but Mary's recollections emanate from her Storer Avenue area home, from the house in which she was born and where she has lived all her life.

The term "entrepreneur"—so popular on today's business scene—was unheard of in those days, but West Side neighborhoods were full of them. As Mary puts it: "There was a butcher on every corner."

There were the major employers, of course. The likes of Republic Steel and Standard Oil. And the breweries: Standard, on Train Avenue; Pilsener of Cleveland (that famous P.O.C.) at 65th and Clark; Leisy's on Vega; and Carling's. Mary remembers that, as a stock clerk at P.O.C., her father made $15 a week. She also remembers she and her brother carried small pails of soup to him for his lunch.

A few women worked in offices, but the textile industry was a major employer of females. According to Mary, "Everybody worked at Joseph & Feiss." That is, if they didn't work at Lyon Knitting Mills.

But everyday neighborhood commerce was conducted by the entrepreneurs.

Mary remembers that, with the soup meat, the butcher "always threw in the bones and liver." In her "Czesky" neighborhood, Otrhalik's Dairy was where sour cream was sold by the pitcher for chicken or veal paprika. You could smell the bread baking at night, she says, and, at the bakery, a fresh housky could be picked up on your way home from an evening meeting.

The entrepreneurial spirit extended to health care in those days, too. The doctor and dentist were "around the corner," says Mary, and "the neighborhood midwife lived on West 52nd Street. One of the kids would always go to meet her when she was coming".

One especially colorful entrepreneurial feature of neighborhood life, in the first half of the century, can never be replaced by supermarkets or shopping malls. To your very door they brought the essentials, those ice wagons, and fish wagons, fruits and vegetable wagons, and milk wagons. The horses were as well known to the community as the tradesmen.

Many share Al Kukla's recollection of the milk wagon horse moving ahead on his own to the next house while the milkman made pre-dawn deliveries to doorsteps. And Mary's memory of children fascinated to find, in winter, that the cream had risen to the top, frozen solid and lifting the cardboard cap way off the bottle.

Then there were the wagons of the scissors and knife sharpeners, who came to fix your sewing machines and umbrellas while they were in the neighborhood. Perhaps the most colorful of all, the ragmen with their distinctive chant, "Rags, bones, bottles..." They took papers, too. In fact, Al remembers that rags were recycled in the Flats, down the hill from West Superior behind the Western Reserve Building, and that there was a "waste paper outfit" as well.

Al remembers too that his own uncle drove a horse and wagon for McClain's, a store supplying feed for cattle and other animals. Which is another reminder that urban life then wasn't quite as urban as we know it today.

Mary used to take the interurban streetcar at W. 65th Street and Detroit Avenue to travel all the way out to her aunt's farm — in Rocky River. Closer to home, she recalls when Storer Avenue was still a dirt road, and the time when, "a young cow got on our street," having escaped from the stockyards nearby.

In that Storer-area home she would wake up to the sound of roosters crowing, for chickens were kept throughout the neighborhood. And her yard was rich in fruit trees; people grew their own cherries, apples, peaches, plums and grapes.

Cookies played a major part in children's lives then, as today. Mary recalls acquiring a big bag for a dime at a store near the West Side Market, while Lucille paid a quarter for two pounds of fig newtons at the A & P at W. 26th and Detroit.

Other neighborhood stores, that have survived in the memories of both Al and Lucille, are a candy store named Manuel's and a grocery store which Al remembers as "Grogan's," and Lucille remembers as "Brogan's." No matter. More than half a century later, the store still lives in its patrons' recollections. It was at Detroit and W. 28th.

Another enterprise both Al and Lucille recall is the "health club run by Finns" on Franklin Boulevard.

Lucille Schnitzer's mother was from Ireland, by way of Boston. Her father was a master mechanic from Mansfield. Lucille claims that, when he arrived here early in the century "he was the only German in Mrs. O'Grady's boarding house".

Lucille's first address was on Church Avenue; she used to play in Mahoney's yard on that street, one she recalls as big enough for three or four houses. Cleveland's Firehouse No. 4 was on that same historic street, and today, Lucille remembers the area as "Precinct 8".

Although St. Mary, the German church, was close by, Lucille remembers going to St. Patrick's as a child. And occasionally to St. Malachi's, where the altar boys, she says, were "rough and ready".

When she was seven, the family moved to West 32 Street, near the Academy of Our Lady of Lourdes, which Lucille attended all through grade and high school. She remembers small classes of about 12 pupils, but when she graduated in 1927, at 17, it was with a "large class" of about 35.

Lourdes then was at West 31 Street and Franklin Boulevard. The convent was in the "old Weideman mansion." (Later it was to occupy the present site of the May Dugan Center.) On Franklin, the school was a block east of what in turn was the old German Hospital, then Fairview Hospital, and now the Cuyahoga County Nursing Home.

Lucille can personally testify that good works have been going on in that neighborhood for a long time. She remembers that the Blue Nuns "fed the poor" and that she and the other children could "look out the window and see the lines".

Like Mary, Lucille traveled on the interurban cars, sometimes as far as Valley City. But for her, "uptown" was not all that far. "Uptown" was the Lorain Avenue and West 25th Street area, with the West Side Market, Fries and Schuele, John Meckes and Sons, and other popular merchants.

OUT
TO EAT

Al, Mary and Lucille all share good thoughts about that particular shopping area, with Mary saying, of the venerable Fries and Schuele's "the people there were so nice".

Brookside Park played a big part in the early lives of Al and Mary. He remembers, among other things, the people lining the hillside on the Fourth of July; she remembers carrying her lunch and marching along with the nuns for St. Procop School picnics there.

"Gymming" was a popular recreation in Mary's neighborhood. So were festivals, card parties and other social events at her own Bohemian St. Procop Parish, as well as at the Italian St. Rocco Parish, the Slovak St. Wendelin, and the Hungarian Reformed Church as well.

Al, who remembers his grandfather's Austro-Hungarian Empire army uniform hanging in a closet, enjoyed, in his youth, the many opportunities for European music and dance. Among his favorites were appearences by radio's Alois Havrila.

Mary remembers going to the Norval Theater on Sundays for 10-cent movies. Lucille, however, occasionally enjoyed more sophisticated entertainment. She was only nine or ten when she saw her first vaudeville show. But not in the neighborhood. It was at the Palace Theater. All the way over on the East Side...
— *Mary Englert*

Going "out" to eat in the middle of the 1900's meant an occasional night out for parents. Maybe they'd go bowling and would get something there; or maybe they'd try a new, exotic place like Chinese; or maybe they'd go to a fish fry at a church or beer joint. If it were fancy, like after dancing or something, they'd go downtown, or maybe to Kiefer's on Detroit.

But kids didn't go to real restaurants with any regularity. In fact, there weren't even many restaurants around. If kids went "out" to eat, it often meant out for a picnic at a park, or supper at a relative's. Relatives often lived somewhere near-by, even if it meant you went by car to get there.

Diney's and Royal Castle's were two of the first fast-food, drive-in type restaurants around the West Side. When pizza parlors started opening up, most of the kids just couldn't wait to frequent the places. They even became a little hang-out of sorts. But when Big Boy chains, followed by McDonald's, started spotting the city, kids thought they really had "arrived." If you could ride up to Memphis, or W. 117th or Berea Road, you could try one of those burgers for 12 cents or 15 cents, advertised so tastily on the radio. To make it even more worth the trip with your friends, you'd order fries and a shake (maybe the fabulous Ghoulardi shake). That was real living.

"Going out to eat" changed radically during the middle of the century — from going over to grandma's to fancy dining at what, in just a few years, would become a maze of eateries, where you could get everything and anything you wanted — except Mom's cooking.
– *H.K.G.*

TO MARKET....
TO MARKET....

And if you're going to buy food, the West Side Market certainly has a variety. Situated at Lorain and West 25th Street, the Market is a place on the Near West Side recognized by most Cleveland area residents. But did you ever wonder about the beginnings of this massive food "shop?"

A special 100th Anniversary publication of the West Side Market tells us that Josiah Barber and Richard Lord, settlers on the Near West Side who owned most of the land through the Connecticut Land grants, were the true founders of "Ohio City." They knew it was not only important to have a market to help build up the industrial and residential area, but that farmers living west of the Cuyahoga River needed a place to bring their goods to sell. In 1840 a gift of land on the northwest corner of Pearl Street

(now West 25th) and Lorain Avenue, was made to the City by Barber and Lord. In 1868, a wood frame structure was built on the site and became known as the Pearl Street Market. This market was used until 1901, when the City of Cleveland bought the current site, across the street from the old market. Construction was begun in 1908 and completed in 1912. A clock tower was also built as a beacon for anyone coming to the market. In 1974, the West Side Market became recognized as a National Historic Landmark.

So, for 150 years, people from the Cleveland area have been able to enjoy the many delicacies available at the Market. . . from bratwurst to pickles, to eel, octopi, caramel corn, etc. Of the 140 tenants and 180 different stands with their families and employees, totalling over

400 people, many are currently fourth generation family operators. The nationalities represented are a mix familiar to the West Side and its residents: Bohemian, Croatian, Dutch, Finnish, French, German, Greek, Hungarian, Irish, Italian, Jewish, Polish, Romanian, Russian, Scottish, Slovak, Swiss, Ukranian and Yugoslavian . . . a variety of Americana.

If you've never been there, you've missed a lot. You not only see a bit of the past, but help share in what is surely the future, for after 150 years, people hope it will always be there! From the hawkers, to the meek little bakery ladies, the West Side Market is a great place to visit, and even better, if you enjoy food!

– *Rebecca Toney*

CSU ARCHIVES – THE CLEVELAND PRESS COLLECTION

JOSEPH & FEISS COMPANY

Traveling across I-90 heading east or west, close to W. 53rd, you can see a huge sign that says"Cricketeer-Geoffrey Beane-Country Britches-Hugo-Boss..."and you know that something great must be made there. There is.

According to the Encyclopedia of Cleveland History (Van Tassel and Grabowski, 1987), in 1845, a clothing firm called Koch and Loeb began at 82 Superior Street. It sold men and boys clothing and was famous for its white summerwear. It also sold piece goods to merchant tailors and retail clothiers. They sold their own brand too, but it wasn't manufactured at the shop. The cut parts were sent out to small ethnic shops—Bohemians put together the coats and overcoats; Hungarians and Germans the vests; and Germans the trousers—sort of an international outfit!

In 1872, Moritz Joseph came to Cleveland as a senior partner of the company. The name became Koch, Goldsmith, Joseph & Co. Until his death in 1917, Joseph was said to be the first person there in the morning and the last to leave at night. Joseph is still remembered as a man who helped to provide for the poor through his charity efforts.

In 1897, the company began its own manufacturing. 1907 brought about the incorporation of Joseph & Feiss Co. With the growing operations, a new factory was built on "Swiss Street" (Now W. 53rd), at the intersection of the New York Central Railroad.

The company met new manufacturing problems by using new methods, machines and scientific management, including time and motion studies. It was able to improve efficiency and cut costs. Employees received higher wages and reduced hours.

A matron was hired to supervise female employees. Further building renovations created extensive dining areas, recreation and sanitary facilities for all. The company became a pioneer in employee relations and benefit packages — it provided health, life insurance and retirement plans.

Pioneering in name identification of clothes was also a part of Joseph & Feiss's past. Their biggest selling item in the early 1900's was a $15 "clothcraft" blue serge suit. It was considered the Model T of clothing.

Joseph & Feiss Co. weathered the war years and continued on. In the 1960's they merged with Phillip-Van Heusen but retained their name. The merger allowed expansion for retail and manufacturing outlets.

In 1990, the company again was sold. It has maintained their name and added new lines, with anticipation of international sales.

The community is proud of Joseph & Feiss Co. It has supplied many jobs and has continued Moritz Joseph's concern for helping the many needy of the area.

– Rebecca Toney

THE HEISMAN HOUSE(S)

Under the leaden skies of November each year, the nation's outstanding college football player is named winner of the Heisman Trophy. The Near West Side has a year-round Heisman commemorative, in the form of a large bronze plaque, on a four-foot pedestal, in front of 2825 Bridge Avenue.

John Heisman, the coach who invented the forward pass, the center snap and other innovations of modern football, was born on Bridge Ave., in what was then Ohio City, on October 3, 1869. He was the son of a cooper named Michael Heisman, who, at various times, had barrel factories on Lorain Ave., and behind the family house on Bridge Ave.

Heisman coached at eight colleges, including Oberlin College and old Buchtel College, now the University of Akron. In 1916, he coached a rampaging Georgia Tech in a 222-0 rout of Cumberland College. But it was not until the 1970's that John Heisman's origins became common knowledge, due to a campaign to have the plaque placed in front of what was believed to be his birthplace.

Whether the plaque is in the correct spot has been questioned. Research into the changes of addresses by Ohio City and later by the City of Cleveland, after Ohio City was annexed, pointed to 2825 Bridge Ave. as the birthplace. While records show that two houses at that site were built in 1913 and 1916, researchers have said it was possible they replaced the original house.

Another property at 4006 Bridge Ave. is a contender as the Heisman birthplace. Cuyahoga County property records for the 1860's show that

CSU ARCHIVES - THE CLEVELAND PRESS COLLECTION

site having been owned by Michael Heisman, with a house at the sidewalk and another structure behind it. But the two houses currently on that lot were likely to have been built in the 1880's, given the styles of carpentry and types of foundations.

What is known for certain is that the legendary John Heisman was born on Bridge Ave. And perhaps it is fitting that we don't know exactly where. After all, among Heisman's contributions to football was the hidden ball play.

— *Tom Andrzejewski*

TEACHOUT
HOUSE*

For twenty years, I have been the happy mistress at the Teachout mansion at 4514 Franklin Boulevard. The house has been a great place to nourish four children and still have room for the extended family, pets, and the many guests who have always been an important part of our busy lives. Times have changed since lumber king and Sunday school teacher Albert Teachout built this house in 1887 and began to rear his family. In those days, they rode in horse-drawn carriages and kept house and grounds, with the help of servants.

Teachout was a friend of President James Garfield. Before he became President of The United States the two would meet to play checkers or to discuss matters of the Franklin Circle Church. To this day, a plaque hangs on the church wall commemorating Teachout's years of service, and a stained glass window which he donated says: "In memory of Abraham Teachout" (Albert's father).

A lover of fine woods, Teachout put a different variety in each upstairs bedroom: birch, curly maple, oak, quartered maple, poplar, etc. Downstairs, each sliding pocket door has beautiful panels, two rooms are wainscotted, and the fireplace mantles, stairway posts and spindles are beautifully carved and detailed. The dining-room floor has five kinds of wood in the design.

By the time we moved here in 1971, the carriage house and gracious curved front veranda were gone, torn down after the tornado of 1953. Only the more private side and rear porches and the two balconies have been kept or restored for our use. But the loss of the front porch does allow more light from the south to shine into our library/music room.

Teachout built our home in the suburban section of Franklin, west of Taylor Street (West 45th St), which was the end of the streetcar line. Rockport and West Rockport (Lakewood and Rocky River) were summer resort areas accessible by the Interurban line which began at W. 58th Street. Detroit Avenue had been a stagecoach route, so had a long history of settlement and commerce.

The seven rooms on the third floor were probably servant's quarters, as the stair leads up directly from the side hall entrance, kitchen and seven-room cellar. We use the third floor as an income suite, so I only have to clean fourteen rooms instead of twenty-one!

For children, this house was a plus; it appealed to the child in us all: a stimulation for childhood fantasies, perfect for the "land of make-believe", costume trunks, and creative imagination.

I knew there was no way that even the most watchful parent's eye could always monitor the activities of all four children in such a house. This wasn't all bad, for I believed in children developing their own initiative, even if that sometimes included mischief-making. Also the house was perfect for "Hide and Seek" (basement off-limits), and a strange game they invented called "Spy vs Spy." They tell me this game is not possible without two stairs.

What else was fun about the house? The back yard fire pole! Every kid in the neighborhood loved sliding from the second landing of our fire escape down to the ground.

Moving here provided a parent with a second important resource. In this place, there was work for everyone. After we restored this house, we bought one down the street, that had once been the home of Mayor Buehrer, began to restore it as elegant rental suites, and eventually fixed more single houses and mansion apartments. Even the little girls could help paint wrought iron fences. The boys were taught to do electrical and plumbing to code by Charlie, a busy State Senator, who had previously been a licensed and bonded contractor.

I've always believed the cruelest thing is not teaching children how to do useful work. So Franklin Boulevard provided quite an apprenticeship. Years later, when Paul, our son, was between college semesters, he took on a restoration project in Victorian Village in Columbus, which he handled all by himself. So he must have learned a great deal here. John, our other son, later did wiring on an entire addition to his grandmother's summer house. So he also learned valuable skills.

We still sit on a Victorian-era Empire style swan sofa; but we hope it's somewhat more comfortable. Yes, we still play chess (and also Pictionary) in the tower alcove of the front foyer. The house at 4514 really has been a joyous place for all of us — a challenge, a historical treasure, and still a place with room enough for our children and all of their friends when they come home.

4514 Franklin Boulevard, home of Alice and Charles Butts

LOST
IN THE
50'S

In 1951, when I was 15 years old, a bicycle was a great means of transportation. We rode from Greenwood playground all over the West-Side; Edgewater, Brookside Park and Fairview at W. 36th and Franklin to play baseball against our bitter rivals, who lived around W. D. Howells Jr. High.

But, as my 16th birthday approached, it was time to take my Press route savings and trade my two wheel bike for something with four wheels. I had my choice of pre-war or post war but when I checked to see what my savings would buy, I knew that a 1950 Mercury Coupe was out of the question. I searched the classifieds to see if my $150.00 would get me something that I had seen in Hot Rod magazine. I finally found the perfect car, a 1932 Ford Coupe; now, all I had to do was convince my father that it was perfect. That proved to be a little harder than I imagined, as he was looking for a car for me too, and his idea of cool was not exactly the same as mine.

"The car doesn't have any fenders," my Dad said.

"That's customized" I said.

"The paint is dull," Dad said.

"That's primer over the body modifications, and besides,

it's channeled 13", I said.

"What's channeled?" Dad asked.

(He had me there)

I guess I missed that issue of Hot Rod.

Finally, after what seemed like forever, he said yes, and the Coupe was mine. I could imagine myself "cruisin" down Lorain Avenue,

the envy of all my friends. I found out what channeled meant the first time I drove the Coupe. It meant that you sat with your legs stretched straight out with only the minimum of a seat to absorb the bumps, that felt like bomb craters, as you passed over them.

Months later, after much work to get it to run just right and several insurance company rejections, I was ready to take to the streets. With the rumble of power that only steel packed Smitty mufflers could produce, I hung a left off W. 41st onto Lorain Avenue and came to a halt in front of T&L's Restaurant. The Coupe was right at home with the other vintage cars that lined both sides of Lorain Avenue. Hudson, Packard, Nash, Studebaker, Kaiser, DeSoto — yesterday's cars with those names still familiar to us now.

Today, we pay to get into Autorama to see cars, that, for the price of the best cheeseburger on the West Side, you could see as you sat in Dineys Drive-In on W. 117th, an endless parade of vintage cars and street rods that made "American Graffiti" look like a mini report. Each car was distinctive and easily recognizable, unlike today's cookie cutter carbon copies that are bland and nameless.

Times change, not always for the better, and I did too. The years took me from the 32 Ford to a 49 Ford to a 57 Chevy, then finally children, middle age and a station wagon.

The 50 Merc I wanted almost 40 years ago? I bought it recently and, of course it's in primer where the modifications were made. I still go "cruisin" on Lorain Avenue, I can still imagine the vintage cars lining the streets. It's not that I'm trying to relive the '50's; I guess, in a way, I never left them.

– Paul Sabo

GONE FISHIN'

Living on the Near West Side meant you had relatively easy access to Lake Erie; Edgewater, more precisely. Edgewater meant swimming, that is, before it became polluted (polio was still a disease to be reckoned with and polluted water was taboo). Edgewater also meant baseball — there were about five diamonds there and, in summer, games were continuous. Edgewater also meant fishing — perch fishing.

If you were a kid in the middle of the 20th century, you could plan a summer's day of fishing with your friends. You knew about bamboo poles, bobbers, hooks, lines, minnow buckets, stringers, and sinkers. That's about all you needed to go fishing, except for worms, which you could easily get out of your yard the night before. You just watered your lawn, moved rocks and stones, yanked some worms up and put them in an old applesauce or beets can or something like that.

Getting up at 6:00 in the morning wasn't so bad. You'd pack a sandwich and thermos, grab

CSU ARCHIVES - THE CLEVELAND PRESS COLLECTION

your gear and start the trek to Edgewater. Others might be walking or riding their bikes, too, all in hopes that the fish would be biting.

You had to know about the "spots" to fish. There were some west of the old bath houses, some to the east, off the rocks. Lots of people might already be fishing by 7:00 a.m., quietly staked out on their rock, line in the water, maybe with a few fish on their stringer. You'd join in, leaving a respectable space from the person already there, careful to judge distances so you wouldn't get your line tangled up with someone else's.

And then you'd sit, watching the water, soaking up some sun, checking your line from time-to-time, chatting with your friend, or reading the comics. If you weren't too lucky one day, there'd be another. After a while — 2, 3, 5, hours, you'd start the long walk home, maybe stopping at Howard Johnson's on Lake Avenue for an ice cream cone.

Such were of the simple, lazy summer days in a big city like Cleveland.
— H.K.G.

ORCHARD
SCHOOL

In 1953, when I was transferred as principal from Observation to Orchard School, the enrollment was about 670 pupils. Within three years, it was over 1000 and continued rising until the number was 1435. Both the Chevrolet and Ford companies were hiring people from West Virginia, Kentucky and Tennessee to work here at their factories. It was not until Paul L. Dunbar School was built that the enrollment decreased.

Many of the children, who came from the southern states, liked the old building, which was built in 1869. The walls were so thick that we didn't have to worry about tornadoes. The beautifully polished wooden banisters looked very inviting for sliding down them when no one was looking. The old wooden stairs made eerie creaking sounds.

Part of the old building was demolished in June 1961 to make room for a new building.

On November 20, 1961, twenty classrooms of pupils moved into the new partly completed school with work crews all around them finishing the construction. There were pupils in the old building, in the Annex built in 1901, and some in the new. It was a little hectic at times, but both the staff and pupils rose to the occasion and we managed beautifully.

In March and April 1962, when the west end of the building was finished, the rest of the classes moved into their rightful places. The old 1869 building was demolished in May 1962. The new Orchard School was dedicated in October 1962.

Many of the children from the south were shy and a little afraid when they came to such a large school. But so were the Puerto Rican pupils who came several years later from Puerto Rico and New York. Fortunately, Orchard had a dedicated staff who did everything possible to help the children adjust to this new situation. Before long, a bi-lingual class was formed to help Spanish speaking children become familiar with English. As principal, I was glad that I could speak Spanish to assist a non-English speaking mother.

My fourteen years as principal of Orchard School were a great challenge to me, but also a time of great fulfillment of hopes and dreams. The latter was possible only because of the wonderfully dedicated staff at Orchard and the tremendous help of a great P.T.A. which assisted in furthering good education for all the children.

All who ever attended Orchard School would admit that one of the greatest influences in their lives there was a teacher named Helen I. Peterjohn. Her 40 years of teaching there was a special gift to all who were privileged to know her. Ask anyone who went to Orchard School between 1926 and 1966.

—*Margaret F. Middleton*

DOOR
SERVICE

In the middle decades of the 20th century, many people eked out a living as door-to-door salesmen. It was rather common, back then, for women to work in the home, so a salesman usually found a captive audience at each door he knocked.

There were insurance salesmen, each having certain 'debits'. There were Fuller Brush men, vacuum cleaner salesmen, even the milkman who'd always be looking for new customers. Salesmen sold books, soaps, encyclopedias, coffees, teas, different salves and ointments. Even fishermen, who caught perch off the rocks at Lake Erie, would have special customers on Cleveland's Near West Side. There was one such kind of door-to-door salesman, however, with a domain all his own.

Some called him the "umbrella" man, or the "scissors repair man", or the "tinker". He pushed a wooden cart, about four feet high, that resembled a flower cart or big wheel-barrel. It had one large metal wheel in the front and two legs of wood in the back. He'd pick up the back end and roll down the street on the wheel. When he stopped, he'd set the cart down.

Most significant about it was the bell that sounded in a regular beat as the man walked up and down street after street after street: dink-dink, dink-dink, dink-dink, on and on in perfect musical fourths. You could hear him coming for houses away, enough time to flag him down, if you needed him to repair something. He sharpened scissors or knives with a grinding stone, which he pumped on his cart. If your umbrella needed a new spoke — voila! He did kinds of patches, other small repairs; could tinker around to fix toasters, sewing machines, buckles, latches, etc.

Time was precious—he worked on the spot, got his fee and continued on, his cart carrying all the supplies he needed, his hands the tools of his trade.

–H.K.G.

SECOND EMPIRE ITALIANATE

The large Second Empire Italianate frame house at 4606 Franklin Boulevard, which in 1867 was number 562 Franklin, is probably the oldest home on the block. Stephen Buhrer, mayor of Cleveland from 1867 until 1871, lived there with his second wife from 1901 until the time of his death in 1907, according to his great-great granddaughter, Barbara L. Messner. Buhrer also had served four terms on city council.

At that time it was a huge mansion for a single family. Now it is divided into five elegant suites of two-bedrooms each, with formal chandeliered dining-rooms in each. There are still fireplaces in each suite except for the third floor penthouse, which commands quite a view of the city skyline and lake. The carriage house had to be demolished in the 1980's.

The downstairs suites have twelve foot ceilings and ten-and-a-half foot windows overlooking a flower garden, and the house is shaded front and back by London Plane trees. An old street lamp provides light in the front garden at night. Inside, the sliding doors and several others have "painted grain" done by hand with a feathering technique, and some of the baths have pedestal sinks. A huge central hall with European wallpaper is dominated by a gorgeous walnut staircase.

For some mysterious reason, the basement has 10 foot ceilings, and a visit there is quite an experience, due to its arched doorways, paving block floors and whitewashed walls. One room was once used as a coal room, but whether other rooms were wine cellar, summer kitchen, or what, is not clear. Some find it a bit spooky to descend so deep into a cool laundry room or storage or furnace room in 1993! Surely, if there had been access, the cellar would have been roomy enough for a stable of horses!

Charlie and Alice Butts, the restorers and current owners, have yet to solve many mysteries about the history of the house. Another question: was the huge room next to the dining room, kitchen and pantry areas really just a china closet? And was that really just a linen room which now seems a good-sized bathroom? Was the third floor used originally as servants' quarters? And, how true is the least credible rumor of all: the story that this mansion was really built for a retired couple with no children!?
– Alice Butts

WILLIAM L. HALLORAN

The day after Pearl Harbor was bombed—December 7, 1941—our nation entered World War II. On the day of the bombing, a Cleveland family, the Hallorans, had a more devastating reality; their son, Ensign William Halloran, had been on the USS Arizona. It had been sunk in the bombing. William Halloran had become the first Cleveland casualty of that war.

According to the Encyclopedia of Cleveland History (Van Tassel and Grabowski, 1987) Halloran was a young journalist, born in 1915 and raised on Cleveland's west side. Halloran attended St. Ignatius Elementary School off West Boulevard. He went on to Cathedral Latin High School and later on to John Carroll University, where he served as editor of the "Shopping News Junior." He transferred to Ohio State University in 1936, worked as staff on the paper and in 1938, received a B.S. in Journalism.

After graduation, he went to work for United Press International, as a reporter with the Columbus Citizen. In 1940, UPI sent him back home to Cleveland, to work for the Cleveland Press. The same year, the world situation was worsening. Halloran felt a need to be a part of helping make things right. He enrolled in the U.S. Naval Reserve Midshipmen's School at Northwestern University. In June, 1941 he received his ensign's commission.

He came home to visit his family at the end of June, then left to begin his duty aboard the USS Arizona, which was stationed at Pearl Harbor.

Halloran was posthumously awarded the Purple Heart; American Defense Fleet Medal; Campaign Medal; and World War II Freedom Medal.

A special memorial service was held for him on December 17, 1941 at St. Ignatius Church, West Boulevard and Lorain. Hundreds of Clevelanders came to mourn his death and the tragedy of Pearl Harbor.

The USS Halloran was dedicated to him in 1944, at the Mare Island Naval Yard, in California. His mother christened the ship.

In 1945, the city of Cleveland dedicated a park in his name at W. 117 and Linnet, near his home. If you pass by the park, you might see kids playing basket-ball, baseball, football etc. in the huge field. But you won't see a statue, or a huge plaque dedicating this land—the name is enough. It denotes the bravery and caring of a young man who loved his country, and made Cleveland proud.

– Rebecca Toney

THE WEST SIDE HUNGARIAN LUTHERAN CHURCH

By the 1930's there were a sufficient number of Hungarians on the Near West Side of Cleveland that a congregation was formed by Lutherans of Hungarian origin. The Reverend Dr. Gabor Brachna, a native of Hungary, and having received scholarship training at Union Theological Seminary, Columbia University accepted a call to augment the spiritual as well as the social needs of this newly-formed congregation.

In 1938 a dormitory building was purchased from John Carroll University on W. 28th Street. It had formerly been the residence of the Schlatter family, who, until Prohibition, had a brewery across the street from 1900 W. 28th Street. Today that residence would have rested where the track and field are for St. Ignatius High School. On the northwest side of the property, adjacent to Joe's Bar across the alley, was the former stable/garage and then gym for John Carroll, which became the church of the West Side Hungarian Lutheran Congregation. The altar, built by church members, is still in use today and can be found at the present location at West 98th and Denison Avenue.

Based upon an interview with the Reverand Brachna, the West Side Hungarians at that time were more adventurous than their counterparts who remained on the East Side/ Buckeye area. They were a mix of first and second generation Hungarians. The first generation instructed the youth to work hard and save to buy property. To the second generation, education was more important.

There were hardships, especially unemployment. Members were afraid of losing their homes. Reverand Brachna said, "It wasn't unusual to announce in church a 50 cents donation." However, there were those who did have jobs as domestics, factory workers, and semi-skilled laborers.

An on-going problem among the Hungarians was that they represented 62 counties in Hungary. Each group kept its willingness to help each other, according to the county. Numerous clubs, social organizations and insurance groups, such as Sick Benefit Societies, arose out of these narrowed interests.

The family unit was strong. Somebody wielded the authority. For instance, in spite of the proximity of Joe's Bar to the church, Rev. Brachna stated, "It never caused a problem, perhaps due to the fact that the wives didn't hesitate to check for their husbands."

Religion and marriage also caused problems. According to the pastor, children born to couples were expected to be brought up in the religion of their father for the boys, and the religion of their mother for the girls.

The West Side Hungarian Lutheran Church had two regular church services (the men sat on the right, women on the left), a choir, Sunday School, youth groups, a Hungarian language school, and drama club for stage performances. There were picnics, banquets, flag-dedication ceremonies, sausage making, Name Day dinners and balls, traditional Easter sprinkling customs and the Grape Harvest Festival during the year.

Several of the men from the congregation served in the Armed Forces, which included the Pacific theater and the Merchant Marine. Many gave their final sacrifice for this country.

By 1944 members within the congregation felt that W. 28th Street was no longer their community. Businesses had taken over much of the property around the church. Many had bought homes farther out on the West Side. It was their suggestion to resettle to W. 98th and Denison Avenue.

– Gabor S. Brachna

CSU ARCHIVES – THE CLEVELAND PRESS COLLECTION

POPS

Back in the 40's and 1950's, soda pop (just called "pop") was an extra special treat for a lot of kids in the Near West Side. Kids liked the basic fruit-flavors, like orange, cherry, strawberry, grape, lime, creme soda, or root beer. There was also coca-cola and ginger ale, but adults usually had that. And there was a grapefruity pop called "squirt", also for adults. Most pops came in short 6-pack, returnable bottles. There were also quart-sizes, also returnables. A small bottle cost a dime; a quart cost a quarter.

Some of the names of these pops included: Birely's (specializing in grape and orange), Dana (all flavors, often found in chest-sized machines like the one at Cudell Arts and Crafts), Lil Tom's (you'd get them in cases for big parties or weddings), Cotton Club (they had everything), Dad's root beer (and later Hires root beer), Canada Dry (mostly gingerale) and the big one, Coca Cola. It was always "coca cola" back then; "coke" came later. Pepsi, although new on the market, was no rival to Coca Cola.

Then soda fountains started to serve nickel glasses of a brand new thing: cherry coke, chocolate coke, or lemon coke. It became a craze. Soon after that it seemed as though the pop market opened up. New pops were popping up every month. There was Get-up, Like, Double Cola, Bubble-Up, Dr. Pepper, R.C. Cola, Fresca, Mountain Dew, Tab, Sunkist, Uptown, and we all tried a few bottles of each. A lot tasted similar to another.

Maybe these brands were around earlier, in other parts of the country. Perhaps the market opened up in Cleveland because of the development of interstates and the whole transportation network. Maybe some pops were genuinely new, and looking back, they've disappeared from the stores, now only a memory.

But to the kids of those times, used to kool-aid and an occasional nickel phosphate at a soda fountain, or birch beer from the Royal Castle's — these new pops were quite the thing to have sampled among your peer group.
– H.K.G.

A FORMER ST. IGNATIUS H.S. STUDENT REMEMBERS THE PAST

There was Heck's. It was loosely called a candy store, but it was a business that catered to the St. Ignatius High School crowd and sold soft drinks (lots of Pepsi) and potato chips to the boys before school, at noon time, and after school. It was anything but "posh". It was crowded, smoke-filled, and noisy. How anybody wanted to eat lunch in there was beyond me! Many did have their breakfast, lunch, and after-school Pepsi there. A real meeting place, a place of easy acceptance, and they always had plenty of what Clevelander's call "pop", and others call soda. It was legendary. There was nothing else, no other store so small, that could attract so many. Nowadays, Heck's is in the same place, has essentially the same building, and I marvel at the size of it and how many people it used to hold, and have passed through its two doors.

Then there was St. Patrick's Church. It was a thriving Jesuit-run parish and drew the total student population at the opening Mass of the school year. There was a hall at St. Patrick's on Bridge Ave. where the St. Ignatius Drama Club presented a yearly play. That hall was the center for sports banquets and dances too. A place where memories were born. Nowadays, St. Patricks is run by diocesan priests and the church is open only on Sundays, but a renovated hall is still the scene of plays presented by the West Side Theatre group.

Then there was a church located at W. 30th and Carroll Avenue. This was the drafty, old St. Mary's Church. Students attended Mass there in the morning and expected it to go on forever, I guess. The bells would ring once in awhile for all to know that this church was there. Its presence was felt as we rushed by it everyday to an even draftier, older building called the Annex, located south of St. Mary's on W. 30th Street. Today St. Mary's is gone. The Annex is a modern building and even the street (W. 30th between Carroll and Lorain) does not exist. It has been removed as a street by the City of Cleveland, and in its place is a mall, a campus for the students. No more crossing the street to get from one building to another.

There were street car tracks right down the middle of Bridge Avenue. Later on, as buses replaced the streetcars, the tracks remained. The same Bridge Avenue is there, but where is Lourdes Academy, an all-girls Catholic school at W. 41st and Bridge Avenue. It was a thriving school, and, if I took the bus early, the girls were all going to Lourdes or possibly St. Stephen's, an all girls Catholic school that specialized in preparing girls to enter the business world as secretaries. It was located on W. 54th Street between Bridge and Lorain.

A legendary gym was located at the YMCA at W. 32nd and Franklin. This gym, a very small one, was the place where neighborhood greats all practiced. Davey Demko, possibly the greatest basketball player in the history of St. Ignatius, was a regular.

The Near West Side was a place where so many people gathered. They lived there. We students were, for the most part, visitors. So many regular sights and familiar names...Father

Barton, a.k.a. "Black Bart", greeting the boys as they came to school and walked past him, day in and day out...Father Sullivan, beloved of thousands of students, who was seen walking across W. 30th to class or to St. Mary's...Fr. Halligan's confession line, the longest in the city on Saturday afternoons. Everyone went to confession to him at St. Patrick's.

There is still one last building still standing, the Carroll gym. There John Wirtz and Fred George began the tradition of great basketball. Yes, in a small gym hardly able to handle a crowd of several hundred. Long before there was a Sullivan Gym it was the starting place. It is there today, a relic, no longer even considered a gym fit for high school events.

Today, the storefronts on Lorain are gone. The gravel parking lot where endless touch football games took place is gone. The dark, soot-stained brick is sand-blasted red, and brand new students ride the buses to 30th and Lorain or 30th and Bridge. They are meeting a place **that is so** different!

I wonder if former students who visit the school are overcome with memories as I am. Do they see the new buildings, new campus, and renovated neighborhood and remember?

King Arthur said in "The Idylls of the King" by Tennyson, "The old order changeth, yielding place to new, and God fulfills himself in many ways." True, so true, of the near west side and the institution known as St. Ignatius High School.

– *Terry Hayes*

CSU ARCHIVES – THE CLEVELAND PRESS COLLECTION

HARRY O

When I was born my Pa, Harry O, promised my mom that he would quit vaudeville. He kept his promise, and, in 1910 opened a dance hall on W. 65th and Detroit called O'Laughlins. Pa never had any formal training as a dancer, but he was sensational.

We lived upstairs from the dance hall. Part of it was rented out to Miss Restler. She was a school teacher by profession, but taught ballet on the side because of her love of it.

When vaudeville acts came to town, Pa would teach them new acts and sell the acts to the dancers. I remember one particular song and dance call "The Tickle Toe" that Pa choreographed. Everyone loved to dance to the Tickle Toe.

When I was in high school, I helped out at the dance hall giving lessons along with Pa. A lot of couples came for ballroom dancing. Pa would dance with the wife while I danced with the husband. In the evening, the hall would be open to the public and the whole family became involved helping out. My aunt would sell tickets at the door, but sometimes she'd be late, so one of the musicians from the orchestra would sell tickets. Vic Buynak was one of the best musicians, and he was always willing to lend a hand.

The one thing Pa would not tolerate was drinking. He used to walk through the hall when it was open to the public and, if he smelled liquor, that person was asked to leave.

Pa also volunteered his expertise to different churches in the area. He helped put on musicals at St. Colman and St. Ignatius.

The neighborhood at W. 65th and Detroit started to change, so Pa moved the dance hall to the Homestead Theater on Detroit in Lakewood. Shortly thereafter, Pa had a heart attack and was confined to bed for a long time. I was married by then, and my husband Bill and the rest of the family tried to keep the dance hall going but it became too much with Pa being sick. We had to give it up.

Harry O was a small man in stature but he had a big heart and a great sense of family. That's how he remains in my memories.

– Margaret Simmerly

I COULD
HAVE DANCED
ALL NIGHT ...

Millions of people, at one time or another, have danced, or longed to dance to the sweet sound of music. According to the Encyclopedia of Cleveland History (VanTassel & Grabowski, 1987), Cleveland has sponsored public dances since 1854. In that year, the dances were the two-step, the waltz, cakewalk, etc. When sheet music became available (around 1910), public parks realized the recreational value of dancing and opened community ballrooms. On the West Side, Edgewater Park had a dance pavilion which overlooked the beach; Brookside Park had a building which used the second floor for dances; and Puritas Springs Park had not only a ballroom, but an outside dance area, as well.

Supperclubs were designed for "proper society" dancing; hotels maintained special clubs for guests of the hotel. During the 30s and 40s, many radio broadcasts were aired directly from these hotel clubs. If you didn't want to dance out, many well-to-do families converted part of their home, usually the third floor, to ballrooms, with special stairs for a separate entrance from the house. Franklin Castle, on Franklin Avenue, has one of these large ballrooms.

Public dance halls and ballrooms were scattered all over the West Side. There was Banater Hall at 119th and Lorain; Botts at W. 25th and Franklin; Brighton Park ("Flappers Paradise") off Denison; Capital on West 65th; Freeman's on West 25th and Lorain; Hanson's at 1900 W. 25th; Harmony Hall, 2515 Franklin; Jiendo Dance Hall at 4105 Clark; Kings Hall at 3241 W. 50th; O'Laughlin's at W. 65th and Detroit; Sommers Hall, 2945 West 25th and Vega Hall, 3025 Vega to name a few. In the 1950's most of these halls were converted from dancing to party centers, roller rinks, bowling alleys or to commercial enterprises.

But one has survived all these years as a grand ballroom — The Aragon, 3179 West 25th. Opened in 1915 as the Olympic Winter Garden, it held dances, sponsored roller skating, banquets, weddings and prizefights. In 1930, new owners took over and changed the name to Shadyside Gardens. A few years later, it was remodeled and named the Aragon, after Chicago's finest ballroom. During the 30s to the 50s, some of the most famous traveling bands visited the Aragon. These bands usually played on Sunday evenings — you could really swing — and dance, from the jitterbug to the ball-in-the-jack. On Wednesday, you could come to the ballroom for Polka Night.

Today, the Aragon holds to the tradition of yesteryear. The dances performed are a collection of the past — a "mixer", the cha cha, fox trot, waltz, rhumba, etc., to name a few. Although the ballroom dancing is now limited to Sunday nights, take a drive across West 25th on that evening for a sight you'll long remember: the splendor of ballroom dancing— from people's long brocade or sequined gowns, to tuxedos, to crinolines under pleated evening dresses. And their faces mirror the joy of the dance.

– Rebecca Toney

1950's
MUSIC

Just as music plays a big part in the lives of today's teenagers, it did the same for the kids in the 50's. I turned sixteen in 1955, when the voices of Bill Randle, Phil McLean, Joe Finan and Tommy Edwards were the heavy hitters on the Cleveland airwaves. Those of us who were really cool (or just thought we were), also tuned in Alan Freed and his Moon Dog Show, which aired at 11:00 P.M. each weeknight. He was a little unconventional and less traditional than his peers, but his music was the heart of rock 'n roll. We never realized then, in our little West Side homes, that we were the fans who gave birth to a giant new American music.

Single records (not albums) were where much of our spending cash went; the Record Rendezvous on Prospect Avenue downtown was "the place" to buy those wonderful 78's. Back then, we used C.T.S. #22 or #25 to get to Record Rendezvous. There were several sound-proof booths where you listened to the songs you would just die for if you couldn't buy them that minute. For 89 cents you got one big, black, brittle record that was subject to cracks, chips, or total destruction if dropped.

Arriving home with those great works of art, one would proceed to play them at least 50 times, while putting your hair up in pin curls, and

calling those friends you would be hanging out with that night. Most of the songs had their share of Doo Wop's, Sha La La's, Oop Shoop's and simple lyrics – no messages or deep meanings back then.

As you flicked on the radio, waiting for the tubes to warm up, you would hear Chuck Berry, The Platters, Elvis, etc. The deejays back then gave you some in-depth info on each artist. I've heard some people say that the 50's were boring, but not for me. I got a little high just dropping a nickel in the jukebox at "T & Ls", the local diner (now Nick's Restaurant on West 41st and Lorain), and listening to the songs that I still enjoy today.

I write this in the first person, as it is my own personal recollection of the "Fabulous 50's."
– *Carol Sabo*

1956

During the 20th century, the Hungarian people were a strong community in the Cleveland area, especially in the Near West Side. It wasn't until late in the century that I was able to really comprehend some of the flurry, within that community, during 1956.

I had a Hungarian friend who lived around the corner. I grew to understand Hungarian ways, as opposed to Czech, or Irish, or German, etc., because of hanging around her house. Her family went to fancy Hungarian dances, took photos of themselves dressed in traditional Hungarian clothes which they wore at get-togethers, and had big dinners at St. Emeric's, at which I sometimes was invited to both help and join the fun. I used to think that Hungarians had a special way about them. Being Hungarian meant being "proud" that you were Hungarian. My Hungarian friends never held it against me that I wasn't of their culture, but I knew I wasn't, in spite of their genuine warmth and effusiveness.

But I liked being around them all. I learned to czardas, loved their gypsy violins, and thought they were the best cooks and bakers — paprikash, dobosh torte, lentil soup, nut kuchens, etc. When they had a cook-out, it was saluna. We'd get un-cut bacon and chop it in chunks, put one on a long stick and hold it over the open fire. As the fat would burn, you'd catch the drippings on fresh bakery bread until it was pretty covered. You'd eat the bread. Then you'd cut off the cooked part of the bacon chunk, put it on bread and eat that. Then you'd repeat the cooking of your smaller chunk of raw bacon. That was saluna — "saluna chutnik," I think.

There were always visitors at my friend's, but some new ones started living there for short periods. These new people didn't speak English.

CSU ARCHIVES - THE CLEVELAND PRESS COLLECTION

(That surprised me; most of the Hungarians I knew were bi-lingual.) My friend told me these people were refugees. They escaped the Communists who took over their country. Her family was helping Hungarians get settled in Cleveland.

That year, many came and moved on. I never got to know any really; they had more important things to do to start their lives over.

But, in 1989, when the Berlin Wall came down in Germany and all the world focused on those nearby countries, I remembered 1956 again. We, in Cleveland, played a vital part in the '56 Communist invasion of Hungary. We helped those who escaped to find freedom and a new life.

And of my friends who shared their homes and gave their support to those refugees, I had fond memories, and I was proud.

"Egaseget!"

– H.K.G.

CUDELL

If you were lucky enough to be able to go to the Old Cudell Arts and Crafts House during the 40's or 50's, you took pride in the fine clay animals, raffia hot plates or baskets, and various other sorts of Art that the neighborhood people made. It was a bustling place of real beauty. And you couldn't help but long to have a dime for a bottle of Dana pop (grape, creme soda, whatever) from the chest-type pop machine that stood near the back door of the place.

This special house had an interesting history.

As outlined in the Encyclopedia of Cleveland History (Van Tassel and Grabowski, 1987), Frank (Franz) E. Cudell was born in 1844 in Germany. He came to Cleveland in 1867. As an architect, he set up partnership with John Richardson, in 1870. The firm was known as Cudell and Richardson.

They were both familiar with Victorian and Gothic architecture. Their experience enabled them to build churches, two of which are St. Stephen's on W. 54th and Franklin Circle Church, both still standing. One of the most beautiful buildings constructed by them was the Tiedemann House (circa 1881). This house at 4308 Franklin Avenue became known as Franklin Castle. It is a large rock-faced sandstone mansion with a round corner tower and does resemble a small, but formidable castle.

But beyond his architectural skills was Cudell's concern for the neighborhood he lived in and his own land, which took up a six (6) block area between W. 98th and W. 100th, situated between Detroit and Madison Avenues.

This area is about 1/2 of a tract of land originally owned by Franklin Reuben Elliott, who built the center of the Cudell House in 1845. In 1860, Mr. Elliott sold the land to Jacob Mueller, a German immigrant, who was a lawyer. In the 1870's and 1880's, the land was comprised of a deer park, orchards and huge flower gardens. In 1889 Frank Cudell married Jacob Mueller's daughter, Emma, and they were given the property as a wedding gift. Cudell remodeled the Mueller House and built two apartment terraces on West 99th and Madison.

Cudell died in 1916, and bequeathed part of his property, except for the house, to the city of Cleveland. In 1917, Emma had the Clock Tower built in the large field area near W. 100th in memory of her husband. At her passing in 1937, the house and remaining properties were given to the city. Some of the original property was opened by the Department of Parks and Recreation in 1939 as the Cudell Arts and Crafts Center. The Center was also known as the West Side branch of the Garden Center of Cleveland. The Center has served as a meeting place for many recreational, cultural and educational groups, and was thought to be one of the first municipally run arts and crafts centers in the U.S.

In 1964, a new brick recreation center and gymnasium was built by the city on the property at 1910 W. Boulevard. For over 70 years, thanks to the kindness of the Cudells, people have found a haven for play, learning and great beauty.

–Rebecca Toney

CSU ARCHIVES - THE CLEVELAND PRESS COLLECTION

CSU ARCHIVES - THE CLEVELAND PRESS COLLECTION

MEMORIES
OF GREENWOOD

1944 was a good year for me.

Eight years old and no longer restricted to the back yard, I was allowed to venture out into the "real" world. A big part of my "real" world became Greenwood playground on West 38th St. and it was to remain so, long into my teenage years. The swings, sand box, teeter totters, monkey bars, sliding board and sprinkler were everything I needed to keep me busy for hours on end. During that time period, the city provided college students to work at Greenwood, to organize activities such as crafts and horseshoe pitching tournaments. There was always something to do at Greenwood, and I found myself drawn there spending more and more time each day.

Greenwood was officially open during school vacation, but less organized activities went on all year long. In the winter, the sewer on the ball field was cemented shut and the field flooded by the city to provide an ice skating rink. I remember racing to the playground after school on the first real cold day of winter to make sure the younger children didn't try to walk through the pond and break the slowly forming ice and ruin a winter of skating. After the rink had frozen solid, it was hockey games on Saturdays with homemade equipment, and skating in the evenings, complete with bonfires for warmth.

In the Spring, the rink was drained .We had to settle for playing basketball until the field dried enough to start playing softball. It was an honor to be chosen by one of the older boys and be able to control the games. We stood at the fringes of their conversations and waited for them to finish their Pepsi's, so we could take the empty bottle back to the delicatessen across the street for the penny deposit.

Greenwood was the starting point for everything we did, whether it was a bicycle trip to Edgewater Park to fish or swim, or to Brookside Park to play baseball. Summer evenings always found a group of us talking about what we had done that day and planning our next adventure. It seemed we never ran out of things to do–we even had a penny black jack game in progress on the roof of the storage building most every evening.

In the Fall of the year, the softball diamond turned into a football field. Game after game was played, until darkness sent us home. In 1953 the face of Greenwood was drastically changed – gone was the ball field and skating rink – replaced by a swimming pool. Somehow it didn't seem to be a fair trade-off, as the pool was only used three months of the year, compared to the year-round use the ball field enjoyed.

In 1955, I left the area and Greenwood behind, along with many childhood friends and fond memories of all the fun we had. When I'm in the neighborhood, I make it a point to drive by Greenwood playground, to confirm those memories of a simpler life and good times that I wouldn't trade for anything.

—— *Paul Sabo*

NEIGHBORHOODS
MID-CENTURY

The end of World War II in 1945 really marked the beginning of a new era in Cleveland neigborhoods. Happy times, baby booms, and a developing economy created a need for more housing, more everything. Suburbs grew like mad, and with them, cars and highways were built to transport people and commerce.

For the regular person living in the Near West Side, few could surmise how the neighborhoods would change in the coming decades. Highways bull-dozed houses, even whole streets. "Chain stores" began to replace the old corner mom and pop stores. They bought in volume, had cheaper prices and advertised big. People were curious about the shiny, new, modern stores. They seemed to have so much more than the little corner ones. Lawsons was an early chain on the west side, competing especially in the dairy business. Supermarkets, too, began to increase. Chains, like Fishers, began to compete against A & P, and Krogers; and Regos pressed the market even more.

Shopping plazas and then shopping centers, began to be built out in the suburbs. Sometimes stores from the city expanded into these new markets, and sometimes they just moved completely into them, totally leaving their old neighborhood roots. City folks, curious about such modern areas to shop, began to try them out. There were big stores, small shops, good prices — all put together like a shopping treasure chest. Big discount stores also began to crop up to compete with dime stores, dry goods' stores, hardware stores, etc. One of the first was Atlantic Mills — the best prices for all of your needs. City stores like Giant Tiger, Robert Hall, Fries & Schueles, Western Auto, among others, had tough times hanging on.

Commerce changed radically after World War II through the 70's. West Side neighborhoods lost their shopping bases; they gradually had to depend upon the suburban malls. Even the last department store on the West Side— Sears at Lorain and 110th–finally gave up in the early 80's. Cut up by sprawling highway systems, losing population and commerce to suburbs, the neighborhoods fell upon tough times.

Somehow, however, that old-fashioned, silent spirit that keeps a neighborhood living, kept on. For all the changes that took place, the neighborhood bounced back—different, as time will do to all things, but back again anyway. New commerce at different nodes surfaced, new people began to populate the area and the neighborhoods began again, ready for another century.
– H.K.G.

OLD
MOVIE THEATERS
ON THE
WEST SIDE

Remember when movies cost 10 cents and kids could get in for 5 cents? That was in the early decades of the 20th century.

—— Fatty Arbuckle and serials played at the old Rialto Theater on West 25th near Bridge Avenue or at the old Franklin Theater between Franklin and Bridge Avenue. The Golden Eagle on Lorain opened around 1910.

—— The Victor Theater at Lorain Avenue and W. 78th St. showed silent movies in the early 1900s. Today it is an antique arcade.

—— The Fairyland Theater at 1884 W. 25th had the first 11' by 14' ground glass screen in Cleveland. It seated 500 people and had its own light and power plant. Music for the silent pictures was furnished by a piano and an organ.

—— The Franklin Theater was between Bridge and Franklin on West 25th, where the Riverview Golden Age Center is now.

—— Remember when they played Banko at the Norval Theater, 5306 Storer Avenue, or when you received free dishes on Friday night at the Marval Theater?

—— The Amphion was another movie theater at W. 25th. and Walton Avenue. That theater was torn down before World War II.

—— The new Madison Theater was opened in 1949 at 9417 Madison Avenue. It could accommodate 1600 patrons. This theater replaced the old Madison Theater at 9316 Madison Avenue. It had been a West Side entertainment landmark for 30 years.

—— The Memphis Theater at 4910 Memphis Avenue reopened on February 24, 1943. "Now, Voyager" with Bette Davis and Paul Henreid was featured on the opening program.

Some other theaters in the area were:

> The Stork at 8410 Lorain Avenue.
> The Cozey at 8924 Lorain Avenue.
> The Empress at 9121 Lorain Avenue.
> The Boulevard at 9900 Lorain Avenue.
> The Garden at W. 25th and Clark.

The many movie theaters of the past were a main source of entertainment to residents of the Near West Side. Wonderful afternoons were spent watching Tom Mix, Abbott and Costello and all the other old-time movie stars. A time to be remembered.

– Grace Campbell
Reference material from Cleveland newspapers.

PHOTO: COURTESY RALPH ABRAHAM

SUMMER
IN THE
CITY

Sometimes, when I smell fresh bread or when the sky is a certain shade of blue, I remember. Not everything, I'm sure, but much of those days before serious school, before jobs, before worry could get in the way of a good time. Summer days at my grandmother's house. Summer in the city.

Back in the 1950's and 1960's, the lines between "suburb" and "the city" were not as clearly drawn as today. True, we shopped in suburban malls, drove to most stores, and bought bread and lunch meat in the grocery store. Those things were different in the city. But I didn't look at differences then as being bad; only different.

My grandmother lived on W. 130th Street just north of Lorain Avenue in a big colonial with a wonderful front porch. Many of the houses on the street were doubles and the fact that some people lived "up" and some lived "down" fascinated me. Best friends could actually live in the same house! Anyway, I spent many, many days visiting in the city.

Shopping was a treat. Gram and I would walk to the corner and buy fresh bread (everyday!) at the bakery; meat at Thomas' Butcher shop; and a treat for me at the novelty shop. What a discovery that was! They had millions of toys and treats you could buy for a few cents or a nickel. My brother always got a squirt gun or caps. I got Nickel Nips. Those tiny wax bottles filled with colored, flavored water that tasted like summer. When the liquid was gone, you could chew the wax and make the treat last all day. They also had wax lips and teeth and mustaches. The wax tasted good when you chewed it. Sometimes I got a yo-yo. Duncan. Colored, clear plastic with flecks of silver in it.

On some days, we would walk to the A & P a few blocks away. The smell of freshly ground coffee will forever mean A & P to me. The floor was wood; not tile, and the store was small, but they sold M & M's and that's all that mattered. Vince, the shoe repair man, was another stop on the shopping route. Mysterious and dark, his little shop smelled like leather and polish. Vince was the first person I met who didn't talk like me. He was from Italy and spoke with a heavy accent. Sometimes he scared me, because I didn't understand what he was saying.

Sundays were ritual days, too. Noon mass at St. Vincent de Paul. We walked through the alley from Gram's, behind all the stores hoping we wouldn't have Fr. Flannagan. After church, we'd cross the street to the Leader Drug store and pick up some ice cream or something for later.

Everyday I spent at my grandmother's could not possibly have been the same, but it seems like it; looking out the bedroom window at the street light through the trees, sitting on the porch in the evenings watering the lawn with the hose, shooting off caps with a rock on the sidewalk, riding or pulling the old wagon down the street, eating waffles with ice cream on top, playing the piano.

I measured my growing up by things I did those summers; Preferring yo-yo's to Nickel Nips; talking to the girl next door instead of shooting caps, going to the bakery alone. Summers in the city. Growing up.
—— *Mary Kay McManamon*

HOUSING
ALONG
THE LAKE

I have worked and/or been a volunteer in the Near West Side since 1976. Public housing has weathered enormous societal changes since its initial construction by the federal government back in the 1930's, when tax dollars were given to providing temporary homes for poor people experiencing hard times. About 1985, a group of residents from Lakeview Terrace embarked on a journey to gain management of their public housing community. Their courage, through the struggles of changing to local control is something to be appreciated.

Lakeview Terrace is an old property, with both family and single apartments. The family units (Terrace Apts.) were built in 1935-1937. Lakeview Tower Apts. were later built for elderly and handicapped people.

The Terrace Apts. for families contain a total of 614 one, two, and three bedroom apartments. The Tower Apts. consist of 214 one-bedroom apartments. The Lakeview Terrace Resident Management Firm (LTRMF) is responsible for managing all 828 units located on 28 acres of land.

Located on the banks of the Cuyahoga, Lakeview is considered prime real estate. Just up and around the river bend is Nautica and other "hot spots" frequented by more of the well-to-do community.

The physical design of Lakeview has stood the test of time. The design resembles the "International Style" of architecture, fashionable in Europe in the 1930's. A view of Lake Erie can be seen from every building, because the buildings were placed in a stair-step fashion down along an 80-foot slope.

Balconies add drama to the buildings and provide additional lake views. (The top floors of the Tower Bldg. provide the best view of the Edgewater Freedom Festival Fireworks!).

Lakeview's Community Center, on the W. 25th Street and north walls, contain murals painted by WPA artists. One mural depicts the colonization of Cleveland with Indians on one side, and Moses Cleaveland and colonists on the other. The other wall depicts Paul Bunyan, legendary creator of the Great Lakes.

At this time (1991) the Department of Housing and Urban Development, the Cuyahoga Metropolitan Housing Authority, and the LTRMF are undertaking a $17 million modernization project of all the family buildings and apartments. This is good. At least an additional 20 years of life will be added to the property by virtue of the modernization effort.

– Cindy Ward

COMING OF AGE

When Dwight D. Eisenhower became President in the 1950s, I remember, as a grade schooler, the hoopla that was involved with a visit he made to Cleveland. Classes at St. Ignatius on West Boulevard were called off for the afternoon, and we all went, in strict lines of two, marching down the Boulevard to line up so we could "see" him ride by in his limo. It was a 1/2 day off.

But when John F. Kennedy ran for the presidency in 1960, it was the first time that a presidential vote really took on any meaning to me. Some of it probably was due to a personal "coming of age". But the rest of it surely was the change that Jack Kennedy represented. He wasn't like the presidents we had all seen or studied. He was young, and modern, and spirited; he was also Irish-Catholic — two thumbs up for a great many west siders who were Irish, and at least one thumb up for thousands of Catholics.

Jack Kennedy made good press not only because he was President, but because he instilled a spirit in people. So, many west siders really kept "tabs" on him, his family developments, his children, his ideas. We knew about his brothers, sisters, parents -- the whole clan.

That is probably why I can still remember that November day in 1963, sitting in class at St. Stephen High School on West 54th when the announcement came over the public address system. It was early afternoon. "Attention. Attention, please. I have an important announcement. We have just been informed that President Kennedy has been shot in Dallas. The President has been shot. I am dismissing classes immediately. Please, everyone, go directly to your home," said the principal.

After the gasps, and tears, everyone slowly got up. The halls were silent, but full of girls walking to their lockers. It was like a fog. As we hurried to catch the Lorain bus, no one knew any details.

The next few days were spent glued to the television to watch over and over the assassination of President John F. Kennedy. We saw the swearing in of the vice-president to step in as president. We saw the entourage at the funeral, the riderless horse, the small son saluting his father's coffin...

He had been our President, and he was gone.

– H.K.G.

IT
WASN'T
CLUB MED

I think "unique" is the right word to describe growing up in the 50's. It was an uncomplicated time that let you be a teenager with just the usual ups and downs to contend with. Being "cool" meant belonging to a club (not a gang), and the dress code was simple: washed-out Levi's which, of course, were pegged, T-shirts and, the most important, the club jacket. You picked colors, a name, and any or all of the kids you liked to hang out with, and you were part of the scene on the streets of Cleveland.

I belonged to the Zorelle's, which was supposed to mean "sisters" in Greek, and our colors were powder blue and black. The summer months found us in powder blue jackets with "Zorelle's" in black script on the back, along with symbols that we dreamed up ourselves. Winter was black suede with a blue emblem on the front consisting of our name, club name and symbols, and a rose. Our beat was Lorain and Bridge Avenues, from West 57th Street to Fulton Avenue.

Friday nights we ventured off our turf to dances at Swiss Hall, Clark Rec., The "C" House, Steelworkers' Hall, and schools in the area. You would always run into other clubs at these events, so we stuck together, trying to look tough and cool. The dance floor was our arena as we tried to out-dance our rivals to the tunes of live bands like Sammy D. or the sounds of 78's on the juke box. The Vastel's, The Turks, The Staletto's and the Sigma Chi's were a few of the local clubs.

Dances ended with the sound of squealing tires, loud dual exhausts and, for many of us, a long walk home. It was O.K. to be on the streets then, to talk to guys who pulled up in '49 Fords, '50 Mercs or customized coupes. The music was loud, saxophones were as dominant as guitars, and the Wurlitzer was as colorful as the sounds it blasted forth.

I can still remember those days. As the sun set, on came the club jacket and a hasty walk to the corner to meet a girlfriend. Another evening of making a bottle of Coke and a bag of chips last two hours, and hoping the owner of the local hangout wouldn't ask us to leave. Putting our last nickel in the juke box to play that certain song for the good looking guy with the D.A. haircut. Of the many moments in my life that I would like to re-live, one would be to walk down Lorain Avenue in my powder blue Zorelle's jacket, hoping to see all the cool kids who were so much a part of my life back in '55 and '56

– Carol Sabo

LOOKING
BACK

Often, now in my middle age, when the early October warmth gives way to the cold dampness of coming November, I call forth an image of the Near West Side that lurks in the not-so-deep recesses of my mind. The scene is from out the upstairs front bedroom window at 2053 W. 87th St. The red brick paving stones in the street would glisten with autumn rain. The street lamp and the fading sycamore leaves would throw weird shadows up and down the surrounding walks, yards, and houses.

Though I was born on the Near West Side, we moved early to Lakewood. Still, I was to return often and, by the time I entered high school, I was in and out of the old neighborhoods on a daily basis. As a young child, I stayed often with my grandparents on 87th St. and moved about the neighborhood with confident ease. I can remember the wonderful aroma and the warm bag filled with newly baked raised donuts from Becker's old Madison Ave. store. There was a fire house on the south-west corner of Madison and W. 85th St. and it was hardly ever spoken of without a memory of the revered Skid Stanton. Although I now know that it is really just around the corner, I can remember how cold and interminable the hike from 87th St. to St. John's Hospital seemed.

The street cars rumbled up and down Madison Ave. out to Cordova in Lakewood on its west end and into the Public Square on its eastern terminus, by going down into the subway on West 25th Street. You could sit on the long, curved back seat and look and/or spit down into the Cuyahoga through the open rail ties. Looking out to the south and up the river valley as the street car moved on its way west along the undergirding of the High Level, it was possible to see many of the old South Side's spires along with the bell towers of some of the closer in churches on the west side. My mother would name them all for us, whenever we came from town. They always seemed then as familiar and, at the same time intriguing, as they seem now.

As time passed, some of these churches took on more significance than being mere curiosities. St. Mary's on W. 30th St. had been closed as a parish church but it remained as a place of worship for the Ignatian student community and as a point of pilgrimage for the people who belonged to the Bona Mors (Happy Death) Society and those who undertook the annual Novena of Grace. We were obligated to go to Mass as a class on a specified day of the week and were assigned very specific places. The young Jesuit scholastics would stand in the choir loft and see who was and was not in their seats. The choir loft could be used for other things as well. It was a wonderful out-of-the way place where you could go and copy homework during lunchtime. It was far less crowded than Heck's for an assignment deadline. St. Mary's was also used by the Gypsy community living in the

SHOPPING

Lorain-Fulton area. It was not unusual to have a class interrupted by the mourners and gypsy strings as a funeral procession made its way out of St. Mary's and up to Lorain St. on the way to its burial place.

In those days, you never heard the stories of how St. Patrick's was built, or, that masts from the immigrant ships held up the ceiling. St. Pat's was the large church that could hold the Student body for the mass of the Holy Spirit always celebrated at the beginning of the year there. It gave an opportunity to walk through the neighborhood and see what was going on during what would normally be school time. A person could watch old Dr. Buchtel at work in his storefront office across from Heck's, as he drove his dental drill with his own foot-power on a treadle.

For years, St. Michael's was simply a distant spire with a gigantic angel hovering over the industrial valley. In 1975, I was assigned there as an associate pastor. The dimming past and brightening present were merged together for me. Old memories and aspirations are constantly replaced with new ones. Now, when I travel in and out of the once more familiar neighborhoods, it is evident that life goes on. Memories are usually selective. Old trials and difficulties are likely to be forgotten. New memories are being forged as life goes on.
– Fr. Thomas Mahoney

The growth in shopping outlets, in the first half of the 20th century, was quite the thing in and around the Near West Side.

A focal point for produce and meats was the West Side Market. Hundreds of vendors, of all nationalities, sold their wares to the public there.

Butcher shops, bakeries, creameries, shoe stores, flower shops, paint stores, and hardware stores were also found throughout the mini-neighborhoods of the Near West Side, from Detroit Avenue and W. 25th, south to Storer, west to 65th and further.

May Company, Higbees, Bailey's, Taylor's, Halle's, and Sterling's were the super stores downtown, mostly stocking clothes and dry goods. Purchases could be home delivered, for free. Sears, on W. 110th stocked many kinds of new appliances like stoves, refrigerators and washing machines, as well as clothes. Speckled in between these "borders," were a host of other stores that are recalled in the minds and memories of Near West Siders.

There was Fries and Schueles and Meckes on W. 25th — favorite dry goods stores of the neighborhood. There was Western Auto, also on 25th, for appliances of all types. Giant Tiger, which came a little later, was kind of a catch-all discount store. There was an A&P grocery store on Carroll; Fishers, around W. 38th, came later as a super-market carrying all sorts and large quantities of foodstuffs. There were Kurtz, Lang's and Watkins furniture stores. There were drug-stores, many family-owned.

Merchants were specialists eager to please the customer, often one they knew personally.
– H.K.G.

SOME
HARD WAYS

There are two special memories that kids growing up in the Near West Side, before and right after World War II, might have indelibly fixed in their minds.

One was the way laundry was done. Most all the regular people did their own. We had wringer washing machines. They were usually white enameled, had four legs (with wheels), upon which rested a large drum for water and the clothes. A wringer, or two rollers, was attached to the top of the drum and could swing one way or another to easily drop the wrung-out, wet clothes into a tub of rinse water. Laundry was pretty much an all-day affair. There was a regular procedure that had to be followed and with the washing machine, you needed two laundry tubs right next to the machine, a hose and cleaning soaps to do the job right. You also needed a scrubbing board.

Once dirty clothes were sorted according to colors, whites, etc., you had to scrub stains, by hand, on a scrubbing board. That was a nasty job, because the scrub board didn't do any work; it was merely a good surface for you to rub dirty spots against, to loosen grime and grease.

When these spots were rubbed out, you filled the washing machine, using a hose hooked up to the tub faucet, added the soap and clothing, and proceeded to let the washer do the "rest" of the washing.

Meanwhile you'd have to fill a tub with rinse water. As the machine worked for 10-20 minutes, you fished out a clothing item with a stick (like an old broom handle) and shoved an end of the soaking clothes through the wringer. Sometimes, you might have to put an item through twice, but eventually, you dumped it into the rinse water. You'd have to rinse the clothes in the water — up and down, up and down by hand and then wring them through the wringer again before you could put them in the basket to take outside to hang on the line. We hung clothes out as much of the year as possible; otherwise, we'd have to hang stuff on basement lines.

With white clothes, there was an extra rinse: bluing. We'd buy this little jar of stuff called bluing that you had to add to the second rinse for whites. It wasn't really bleach, but somehow made whites look brighter. It wasn't so bad to help with the white laundry; making blue water broke up the monotony.

Thousands of people have stories about getting fingers stuck in the wringer. Once it started to grab something — clothes, fingers, etc. — that wringer "had" it. People told stories of whole hands going through the wringer. Some even had an arm go through up to the elbow! There was a certain way to release the wringer, but often, emotions took over, when someone

BROKEN
COOKIE STORE

was "caught", and you didn't react fast enough. Eventually, the victim was released.

What is most memorable about laundry is that it was long; then you'd have to iron everything.

Another big memory, for many of us, was coal furnaces. Coal furnaces had no brain to tell them to start-up each morning; that depended on the person who went down into the freezing basement and shoveled coal out of the coal bin, and began to stoke up a fire in the large metal furnace or boiler. Asbestos usually covered the furnace, so you didn't burn yourself if you'd brush up against it.

It usually took an hour to warm-up a home with a coal furnace. Most of the time, the heat was good for about a half day. You had to make another fire for evening.

It was the custom to get coal delivered by the coal truck in summer. Most houses had a coal bin in their basement. It actually was a little room, about 6' x 10' or so, and was always located in the vicinity of the furnace. Coal trucks would back up to a little basement window in the coal bin. The window swung upward and inward and would be hooked up for the coal chute from the truck to fit through. Then the coal would be dumped into the bin to fill the room, hopefully enough to last the winter.

Maybe it was the excitement that automation and electronics brought, with automatic washers and dryers, gas furnaces, garbage disposals and such — or maybe it was the relief we all felt when such new ways made work easier. Whichever, thinking back on those old ways of doing clothes and keeping warm can make you shake your head and cry "yippee!" for progress.
– H.K.G.

Tucked into a little spot, up a flight or two of steps at Carroll and West 26th, was a little store with bare wooden floors, named R & B's. It was the "outlet" store of R & B Biscuit Co. Most people simply called it the broken cookie store.

Oh, they had regular whole cookies, too. But for many people who were poorer, had large families, or just couldn't pass up the bargain, R.B.'s was a real find. If you were shopping at the West Side Market, a stop at R.B.'s easily made sense. You could get a bag of broken cookies for 5 cents–about a pound or so.

It was quite a place. There were counters along the walls. Behind the counters were shelves with stuff on them. The whole store wasn't very big, but space was used to the max. Barrels, each loaded with half cookies or cookies with chips broken off, were all neatly lined up in the middle of the floor. You could look through little glass windows to see the different types. They always had those windmill cookies with almond pieces, and oatmeal ones with icing. There were big gingersnaps, macaroons, raisin, white sugar, and peanut butter cookies. They had butter cookies, bar cookies, jelly cookies, chocolate cookies and cream-filled wafers. They had candies too.

R.B.'s wasn't just a store that provided good buys. To the child in all of us, it may have been the closest thing to "a vision of sugar plums that danced in their heads".
– H.K.G.

CHURCHES—
A LEGACY
OF CULTURES

...Climbing the greased pole at St. Rocco's...admiring the beautiful architecture at St. Stephen's...attending Christmas services at Wesley Methodist Church...or Easter services at Trinity Lutheran...churches were a focal point in the immigration process in Cleveland and an integral part of the community. They were a drawing point for all ethnic people and ethnic pockets formed around churches. Churches stand today as part of the riches of our history, filled with memories of the past, and hope for the future. They continue to meet the spiritual and social needs of the community they serve. St. John's Episcopal Church still stands on West 28th and Church Avenue as Cleveland's oldest church building. The church opened in 1838 and once served as a final stop on the underground railroad. In the 1920's, Italians settling on the West Side put down roots around St. Rocco's (Fulton Road) and later the area of Our Lady of Mt. Carmel (Detroit and W. 67th). Although predominantly Italian, the yearly carnival and procession at St. Rocco's has become a tradition for all groups of people. The Protestant Hungarians had been chartered in 1906 and had services out of a small church on the corner of W. 25th and Monroe. In 1908 they bought from the German community their new church, the Hungarian Reformed Church, on W. 32nd & Carroll. St. Emeric Church just behind the West Side Market on West 25th overlooking the Flats, was constructed in 1925 to attend to the spiritual and social needs of the Catholic Hungarian people. Hungarians continued to settle in the area after World War I and again in the 1950's. Irish immigrants found community at St. Patrick's on Bridge Avenue, which opened in 1853, at St. Malachi's (1865), at the Old Angle and further west at St. Colman's (1880). Many Irish found work at the docks at Whiskey Island, and the close community found it easy to walk to work. German immigrants found similar community and comfort at the old St. Mary's Church and St. Stephen's Church on West 54th. Franklin Avenue Methodist Church, and St. Paul's German Methodist Church were merged in 1947 to form Wesley Methodist Church. Farther west, on West 65th, a Dutch congregation formed in 1890. They met on W. 61st and Lawn Avenue. In 1918, they built Calvary Reformed Church on W. 65th Street. Slovaks built St. Wendelin's on Columbus Road in 1903. Their next-door neighbors in Europe, the Bohemians, founded St. Procop's on W. 41st in 1872.

Churches played a huge part in the development of the community. They are centers of human and neighborhood growth.

– Patricia Ehlen-Milenius

CSU ARCHIVES – THE CLEVELAND PRESS COLLECTION

"SOLID
AS A ROCK"

On any given day, you might walk by the May Dugan Center on West 41st and Bridge Avenue and note what a newer building it is. It's nice-looking — three stories of brick, big windows, modern architecture and a spacious lawn. You'll also notice right along-side the "patio", a huge boulder! This boulder covers about 12 square feet and it's been there, for a long, long time.

According to the Encyclopedia of Cleveland History (Van Tassel & Grabowski, 1987), the granite "rock" is believed to have originated in Canada during the "Glacial Age", between 6,500 to 9,000 years ago, and was part of a glacial advance which resculpted the Cleveland geology.

Pretty impressive!

But it's more special than that . . . If you look closely at it, you will see the following inscription:

HERE STOOD A SCHOOL
West High School 1885-1902
Cleveland Normal School 1903-1909
West Commerce High School 1909-1929
William Dean Howells Jr. High School 1929-1940
Lourdes Academy 1944-1970
Lourdes / St. Stephens High School 1970-1971

The above special imprint was inscribed/dedicated in April of 1989 by the remaining living class members of West Commerce High School. Why, you might ask? In memory of a joyful past

. . .from class pictures taken on or around the rock, to eating lunch with a friend on it, to just hanging around it with friends and contemplating life, and more .

The rock also signifies that today, over 100 years of educational programming has been carried on—from the above-mentioned schools to the adult education classes presently located at the Center. The Center is proud to have the rock as a solid piece of the past that will maintain memories for the future. We will continue the history of educating and enlightening people to all that can be learned in life.
– Rebecca Toney

MEMORIES
OF YOUTH

Moving to Cleveland, Ohio from Canada, in 1955, was a very big move and very long trip. What now is a pleasant five hour trip was, at that time, nine to ten hours by car — a very long time for three children ages six, seven, and eight years old. Our father had a job at The Astrup Awning Company on West 25th Street.

My strongest memory of that area was a place called Rizk's Delicatessen at West 25th and Seymour. You could always count on a man named Eddy to make you laugh when you walked in. There were about six stools in the back of the store at the bar and some tables and chairs, where you could sit and have pop and chips. Eddy always had a joke or a funny story for the kids and lots of penny candy. If I remember correctly, Eddy would sometimes "forget" to charge us. Rizk's would sometimes be a stop for us on Saturdays, while we were waiting for the show at West 25th and Clark to open. We loved to go there. I think we saw "The Seventh Voyage of Sinbad" seven times. Then the Lyceum Show started giving out numbers as you entered. Between movies, there was a car race on the movie screen. If the car with your number won the race, you could go up on the stage to claim your prize. I remember the excitement I felt when my little brother won — but I can't remember what he won.

Going to grade school at St. Ignatius and high school at Lourdes Academy leaves me with many fond memories of the west side.

Walking took up most of our time. From our home at West 91st between Almira and Denison, we would think nothing of walking to wherever we decided to go for fun. It might have been Kiddieland on Memphis, Edgewater Park, Sears at W. 110th and Lorain, The Variety Show at W. 117th and Lorain, the Rollercade, or to my best friend's house on W. 98th and Macon. Walking was just something we all did. It never entered our minds to ask our parents for a ride.

A big treat, if we had little allowance or babysitting money, was to have a birch beer in a frosted mug at Royal Castle or buy cheese curls at Sears–10c worth or maybe even 20c worth.

Many memories are coming to mind as I'm writing this....

Laughing with girlfriend, Connie, as we were trying to walk home from school in snow so deep it came to our thighs. Each step was a difficult task.

Stopping at the candy store on Denison for a cherry coke at the counter and buying some penny candy on our way out. The candy lipstick was my favorite.

May crowning at St. Ignatius — every student had a rose — if a boy liked you, he'd give you his rose.

CYO football games at Thrush Field.

The Bike Shop on W. 99th and Lorain and all the shiny new bikes they had in the window.

The Show Wagon that came to the empty field on West Blvd. every summer with kids as the entertainment...

Stopping at Dairy Dell across from the school on Fridays.

As we got a little older....

Walking down to W. 98th and Lorain Avenue every morning to catch the CTS bus to Lourdes Academy. The bus was full of kids going to St. Stephen and St. Ignatius, as well.

The aroma as the bus passed Laub's Bakery.

Stopping at Ripcho Studio to have school pictures taken.

The warped steps at Lourdes and trying to make it from the ground floor Home Economics room up three flights of steps to the Science room.

The always smiling face of Sr. Mary Terence, Lourdes Academy Principal – she won Principal of the Year award our junior and senior year in a contest on WHK — kids sent in her name over and over again.

Listening to the jukebox at lunch time in the Lourdes Gym, and dancing to fast songs (Paul Anka, Bobbie Rydell, Frankie Avalon, Connie Stevens).

Hurrying home from school to watch American Bandstand.

Playing chess in Roman's Restaurant, on Lorain, near W. 99th St.

Standing on Lorain and West 41st, waiting for President Kennedy to come driving by. The motorcade came to a halt right in front of us so the President could meet our religion teacher, Sr. Ann Cecile, the sister of a congressman.

Although I have lived on the Southeast Side for the past twenty years, since marriage, the West Side has always had a special place in my heart, and I love going back to "the old neighborhood" now and then. It was a great place to grow up!!

—— *Marnie Fell Cravens*

MY LIFE
ON THE
NEAR WEST SIDE

I was born at City Hospital (presently Metro) and was raised on the Near West Side. I lived across from Lincoln High School and watched the high school children practice band and football, when I was a little girl. I remember the milkman with the horse-drawn truck, the ice man, the paper rags man, who always gave me a shiny new dime and a big smile, the umbrella man who sharpened knives and scissors, and the monkey grinder, who played us a tune. I attended Buhrer Elementary School and Thomas Jefferson Junior High School.

Little did I know that after graduating from West Technical High School, I would be attending Lutheran Hospital School of Nursing, at West 25th and Franklin Boulevard. It was my pastor, at Redeemer Lutheran Church at West 30th and Walton Avenue, who influenced my choice of Nursing Schools. I entered Lutheran Hospital School of Nursing in September of 1957 and spent three busy, exciting years with twenty-four classmates, who had the same goal of becoming registered nurses. I have many good memories of those years... My first real patient – quite different than "Mrs. Chase" our mannequin... My first administration of an injection – we practiced using sterile water injections on each other. Working in the Operating Room - that first incision made most of us feel faint (some did faint).

After six months of training, we reached our first goal of receiving our nursing caps, at a beautiful ceremony held at the Historic Trinity Lutheran Church at West 30th and Lorain Avenue. It was truly an impressive ceremony.

I also remember the delicatessen store at the corner of Fulton Avenue and Franklin Boulevard, across from the nurses residence, where the Foundation Building is today. We used our "spending money" for snacks, etc. One of my upperclassmen eventually married the proprietor's son.

Another memory is Andy's Barber Shop, which was located on Franklin Boulevard across from Lutheran Hospital (the site of the present physician parking lot). I'm sure Andy heard many Lutheran Hospital tales from employees and physicians.

In our "leisure" time, which was few and far between, we travelled across the Cuyahoga River to Downtown Cleveland, where we attended a movie at the Palace or State Theaters. Following the movie, we stopped at the "Purple Tree", located in the Manger Hotel at West 13 and Chester Avenue. We were facinated by the "tree" which grew inside and the black light which caused everything white to glow. Today the hotel is gone, but the building houses a restaurant in its place.

After completing our three years of training we graduated, took state board exams and all passed! Upon finishing the exam, we had felt it was impossible to pass!

My classmates dispersed all over the nation, but I still keep in touch with the majority of them. We often reminisce about our experiences at Lutheran Hospital and the surrounding area. One of my classmates and I have remained at Lutheran Medical Center since our training and have seen many changes occur in the hospital and the neighborhood. Most of the changes are for the better, but I still enjoy reminiscing about life on the near west side in the late 1950's.
—— *Barbara McMahon, R.N.*

ST. STEPHEN SCHOOL DAYS

My mother attended school there. My parents were married there and although we didn't live in the neighborhood, we belonged to St. Stephen Parish. From September 1952 until June 1960, I was enrolled at St. Stephen Grade School, 1954 W. 54th Street. Let me share some childhood recollections with you.

The original school structure was ancient. It had high ceilings, wooden floors and steps that creaked and groaned when walked on. The long, tall windows had to be opened and closed with a long wooden pole that hung from the ceiling molding, when not in use.

Each classroom had a huge bulletin board that served as a partition for the Cloak Room — walls studded with brass hooks for students' outer garments. Cigar boxes were provided for short people (myself included) to rest their feet upon.

The primary reader was a rectangular, wedgewood-blue, soft cover book that contained pictures of a boy, girl and dog and those oh, so famous words. "See Jane. See Spot. See Spot Run." Handwriting was a major part of the curriculum. Only in a Catholic school were letter grades given for penmanship.

The teachers' most important educational tool was THE POINTER — a long, blond colored wooden stick with a black bullet-shaped point, used to highlight a word or whack a few knuckles.

In 1953, my second grade class was introduced to the DIPHTHONG (whatever that is) as PHONICS became part of the new reading program.

Outside the new addition, completed in 1953, stood a telephone pole with a huge yellow whistle topping it. It was the AIR RAID SIREN. When it sounded, all students immediately fell to their knees, bent forward, rested their heads on the left forearm while the right arm encircled the back of the neck. To this day, I don't understand how this awkward position was going to save us from THE BOMB and radiation fallout!

It was shiny. It was brass. It had a black wooden handle. It was THE BELL — hand-held and rung by a chosen student-of-the-week to signal RECESS and LUNCH, the two favorite subjects of the day. The asphalt parking lot was divided into the BOYS playground and the GIRLS playground and never shall the two meet — or else! The most popular playground games were Red Rover, Double Dutch Jump Rope and Keep Away.

The cafeteria was in the basement of the old building, equipped with long butcher-block type tables, topped with speckled linoleum and long benches. Metal milk crates, filled with mini glass bottles of chocolate and white milk, stood stacked by the door. The lunchroom lady collected blue milk tokens and red hot lunch tokens. The aroma of huge vats of Mrs. Volpi's macaroni and cheese and trays of warm apple crisp filled the air. The "click-clack" of the good Sister's metal Clicker sounded, as she patrolled the lavatory line and the waste cans.

The good Sisters of Notre Dame staffed the school. They wore the habit — pleated horseshoe veil, black serge cape and long skirt, black stockings and "old lady" nun oxfords. They were excellent educators, had eyes in the back of their heads, were ageless and would never sweat!

SAINT PATRICK'S - BRIDGE

I can remember Sr. Mary Josetta, Sr. Mary John Michael, Sr. Mary Florisita and Sr. Mary Benedictus. Monsignor Joseph Gertz was the pastor, Mr. Hughes was the custodian, and Mr. Weigle was the church organist.

The grade school years were highlighted by several special occasions — First Communion, Confirmation and — the Annual St. Stephen Fall Festival! Tickets were 25c a piece or 5 for a $1.00. Every student was required to sell ten books. The auditorium in the high school was transformed into a casino. The booths were manned by the men of the Holy Name Society and wheels of fortune would spin until midnight the whole weekend. Stuffed animals, large and small, ceramic vases, flower arrangements, home-baked goods by the Altar and Rosary Society — the list of prizes was endless and to a wide-eyed youngster, it was heaven!

Oh, if only those happy days lasted forever. Not so. The culmination of eight years at St. Stephen Grade School ended the first Sunday in June 1960 — Eighth Grade Graduation. As we walked down the long aisle of the church to receive our diplomas, we said goodbye to childhood, each other and the 1950's and said hello to the teenage years, the 1960's and high school — but that's another story!
—— *Paula Margoci McClain*

The Cleveland Diocese was only six years old when St. Patrick's Church, mother church of the West Side, was founded by Most Reverend Amadeus Rappe on July 2, 1853. The Very Reverend James Conlan, Vicar General of the new diocese, educated in Ireland, was appointed as first pastor of the new parish. Two lots on Whitman Avenue (now the site of the grade school) were purchased, and upon them was built a brick church in which the first Mass was celebrated on Christmas Day, 1853.

During the first year the church housed the boys' school, at first taught by lay teachers. Shortly after that, a one-story brick building was built for the boys. The girls' school, opened also in 1853 in temporary quarters at Franklin Circle, was the first school taught by the Ursuline Sisters outside their convent walls. The Reverend Michael Kennedy came as first assistant to the parish in 1854. The next year the Brothers of Mary came to teach the boy's school. The church was consecrated November 29, 1857. In 1863, the girl's school was removed from the Circle to the lower floor of Temperance Hall, a newly- constructed parish building just west of the church on Whitman Street, with one class temporarily in the one-story brick building east of the church. The church property on Bridge Avenue was bought in 1870. A new sixty five thousand dollar school was opened in 1891.

The pastors were: Reverend Eugene O'Callaghan, Reverend Timothy Mahoney, Reverend Patrick O'Brien, Reverend James O'Leary, and Reverend Francis Moran.

SAINT COLMAN

All these priests had helped raise money for the church and school and expanded the parish. The people of the parish were of the working class, mostly poor, with large families. Attending church services was the main part of their social life.

The greatest work of Fr. Moran was the Catholic Club built in 1903 for his young people. In 1913 he added the sanctuary, sacristies, the tower, and stained-glass windows. St. Patrick's is built entirely of rough stone blocks in the Gothic tradition, with a great square bell tower rising over its recessed main entrance. Smaller towers forming the corners of the facade tend to offset the narrowing effect produced by the steep sloping roof. The top of the central tower is heavy with smaller towers and turrets, giving a slightly flattened effect to the open belfry beneath, which houses eleven bells. High over the white marble main altar, lighting the marble-floored sanctuary with rich color, are long windows enclosing within their Gothic mullions, stained glass representing Saints Augustine, Gregory, Ambrose, and Jerome.

– Natalie Cravens

The present Saint Colman Parish was founded in 1880, but even before 1870, a site for a church had been purchased at the corner of Gordon Avenue (W. 65th) and Bayne Street (Wakefield Avenue). When the little property was sold five years later, proceeds were contributed to St. Patrick's, the mother church. It was established as a fund for a new parish, because the population was growing rapidly. The Reverend E.M. O'Callaghan, then pastor of St. Patrick's, voluntarily resigned his office, in order to assist the new undertaking. The first Mass was said for the parish on July 25, 1880, in a one-room frame building on Pear Avenue. A few weeks later the parish school was opened in the little building. In July, 1880, two lots were purchased on Gordon Avenue. A frame church that seated nine hundred people was built on this property. Mass was celebrated in the new church on September 26, 1880. The Sisters of St. Joseph took charge of the school. Additional lots had been added to the church property and when Fr. O'Callaghan died in March, 1901, the parish owned a dozen city lots, while it's membership had increased to more than five hundred families. Most of the parishioners had good jobs and were considered wealthy at the time. The parish had no debts and eleven thousand dollars was on hand for future development.

The Reverend James O'Leary, who succeeded Fr. O'Callaghan on June 30, 1901, was a great builder. He was Pastor of St. Colman for twenty-one years. He built a twelve room brick school, the great stone church, and brick convent besides purchasing lots to carry the parish property to Lawn Avenue. The church was consecrated in 1928.

St. Colman church is built of Indiana limestone, in a free adaptation of the Italian Renaissance style. Guarding the ramparts, on either side of the long flight of steps on either entrance, are recumbent symbolic figures of an ox and a lion, with upright statues of an eagle and a child. The interior is marked by a lavish use of Italian marbles in the carved altar. Particularly interesting are the Stations of the Cross, which are colored mosaic marbles in large rococo frames. The proudest possession of the church is its baptismal font. Its pedestal of Connemara marble was quarried in Ireland and carved and set by Irish marble workers.

—— *Natalie Cravens*

CSU ARCHIVES – THE CLEVELAND PRESS COLLECTION

SAINT MARY'S ON-THE-FLATS

St. Mary's on-the-Flats, whose frame building stood for almost half a century at Girard and Columbus Streets, no longer exists, but its record and traditions, and the many Catholic congregations that were cradled there, then left to build larger and more beautiful church structures, will keep the spirit of Cleveland's first Catholic church alive as long as Catholicism exists in northern Ohio. The church was named "Our Lady of the Lakes" by those who established it, but was popularly known as "St. Mary's on-the-Flats." The original title was almost forgotten even by its congregation.

There were no Catholics in Cleveland until work on the canal brought a large number of Irish here in 1825. When Bishop Fenwick of Cincinnati heard that there were many Catholics in Cleveland and no priest, he had a Dominican priest, Father Thomas Martin, sent to the city in the fall of 1826. Father Martin, and Father Stephen Bodin (the first priest ordained in the United States) visited Cleveland, at intervals, for many years. They said Mass and administered the sacraments in private homes or in the Masonic Hall, the only auditorium large enough to accommodate the faithful. In 1835 the Reverend John Dillon, who had been recently ordained, became the first resident pastor. The people loved Fr. Dillon, because of his enthusiasm, his hard work, and his scholarly nature.

Even Protestants, who got to know him, admired and respected him. Services were held in Shakespeare Hall, then a cottage on Erie (E. 9th) Street and later in Mechanic's Hall, while Fr. Dillon was working to accumulate a building fund for a church. Most of the Catholics of that time were of the laboring class and poor, so Fr. Dillon also appealed to his friends among the Protestants both here and in New York. He finally accumulated a church fund of $1,000. In October, 1836, Father Dillon died at the age of 29, and was buried in Erie Street Cemetery.

Until the present Cathedral was dedicated on November 7, 1852, St. Mary's on-the-Flats was the Diocesan Cathedral. The little church on the Flats was given over to the German Catholics.

From 1850 until 1886, St. Mary's was used as a place of worship for many Catholics of different nationalities. The church had been rapidly encircled by factories. Many nationality churches started being built. On January 6, 1886, the last High Mass was said at St. Mary's on-the-Flats, with snow blowing, both through the crevices in the roof and the broken windows, to chill the large audience of former parishioners who had gathered in the still loved ruin, for the last rites. This was the first time that a Catholic Church in Cleveland was closed and the property abandoned. The last of the old building was razed in 1888. The heirs of the grantors of the land sued for a reversal of the title because the site was no longer used for a church. The property was sold by court order and proceeds were divided equally between the Diocese and the heirs who had brought suit. The original building of the first Catholic Church is gone.

– *Natalie Cravens*

MILES
OF
WALKING

Although the Near West Side "neighborhood" consisted of many mini neighborhoods—some springing up around churches, some around shopping blocks, some around landmarks like the stockyards, or car barns, or parks, even a favorite tavern or playground—it was easy to get beyond your little neighborhood out into anywhere you might want to go throughout the Near West Side. Streetcars and buses took a person just so far through the streets – if you had the money to ride them.

For thousands of people, the best way of getting around was walking. For better then half of the 20th century, most people were lucky to have a car. If a family had one, dad often took it to work. Mom shopped, banked, did doctor and dentist appointments, by foot, or at least walked to catch a streetcar for farther-away needs. Kids— they always walked. Sometimes they could bike.

All kids walked to school. They walked to church, to sport events, to music lessons, to scouts, to dances, to a show, to shop, to skating, to their friends, to get ice cream, to the drug store, to go fishing, to wherever. Growing up in the Near West Side, you could walk from 25th to West Boulevard and not blink an eye. You could walk from 65th to 117th, or from Denison to Edgewater, or from Bridge to the zoo and it wouldn't phase you. All you had to do was leave early. It was as simple as that.

Walking four or more miles a day was the way life was. Maybe not everyday, but lots of days. And the more you walked, stopping to pick-up friends, the more little streets and alleys and stores and places you'd find. So you'd know, or remember, streets like Sackett, and Daisy, and Wakefield, Vega and Gambier, and Jasper, and Western, and Willard, to name a few. Walking made everything seem so close, even though it was miles away.
– H. K.G.

THE
OLD
NEIGHBORHOOD

Red brick-lined streets, houses clad in wood or asphalt siding and built so close together they were "a spit-ball throw away". That was my old neighborhood — W. 103rd between Madison and Western — West Blvd. area. Although the houses were architecturally different, they had one common feature — a big front porch. This is where the neighborhood "lived" and where the kids of the 1950's did most of their growing up. I remember when...

Every summer morning I'd sit on the railing and call "Oh, Francine, Oh, Francine". Fran would appear and together with my sister, Sally, we would plan the day's activities. Playing house was our favorite. From inside the house, we would drag out everything but the kitchen sink, section off the porch into "rooms" and designate who was to be the mother, sister and baby. Finally, we would bribe one of the neighbor boys with "hard candy soup" to be the husband and father. We would play for hours.

The front porch was also a haven for teenagers. I can remember my sister, Wanda, sitting on the old wicker davenport with her girlfriends, listening to Buddy Holly on the radio, setting each others hair in "spoolies" and fantasizing about James Dean and Bobby Darin.

In those days, we walked everywhere. The Madison show on 95th street was 25c for the Sunday matinee. Rose Drug store was on the corner of West Blvd. and Madison. St. Ignatius Church stood on West Blvd. and Lorain. At least three times a week, someone's Mom needed bread, milk or lunchmeat. Hand in hand, we'd make the trip to Vince's (later to become Losers — 103rd and Western) the old corner store. To a small child, the trip was an adventure. "Don't step on a crack, you'll break your mother's back".

Run, walk, skip, race to the corner! Once inside the store, we'd place our order and then make a bee line for the candy case to spend the change on dried, salted pumpkin seeds, pastel-colored candy pills or red licorice.

The summers were always hot. We ran barefoot through the grass, watched the "gypsies" dance on the steaming slate sidewalk and would squirt each other with the garden hose to cool off. Lemonade was 5c a glass and powdered sugar waffles were 10c at the neighborhood lemonade stand. Roller skates were metal and attached to our shoes by adjustable clamps at the toe. Skate keys were worn on a string around our necks. Babies were pushed by older siblings in blue and white "Taylor Tots".

No summer would be complete without Fourth of July fireworks. The next door neighbor would shoot off his shot gun while the children paraded around with sparklers and punks.

In the winter, people kept to themselves. The scrape of a snow shovel against the cement driveway or the purr of the old woody station wagon warming up to take the family to church, were familiar cold-spell sounds.

It's good to remember. It makes me smile, laugh and sometimes cry. It is often said that "You can't go home again", you can't relive the past — but I can — in my mind's eye I can go back to the old neighborhood and I can see, hear, feel and remember good times and good friends. Thank God, for memories!
— *Paula Margoci McClain*

A SPECIAL CLUB –
A SPECIAL PLACE
AND TIME

Cleveland's West Side has always been home to my husband and me. He grew up on West 38th off Chatham, and I on West 47th Street, off Lorain. As the "fabulous 50's" drew to an end, Carol Kopec married Paul Sabo, and a few years later moved to Fortune Avenue, where we have lived for 26 years.

Often, we go back to our old neighborhood, to St. Stephen's church, the West Side Market, Heck's Cafe, and a few of the original stores that still remain. The changes in the area tarnish some very special memories, but yet I still feel drawn to the streets and familiar scenes of my childhood. Time does much to alter the physical appearance of people and places, and nostalgic moments can only be relived in your mind and heart.

I enjoyed growing up on the Near West Side, when "hanging out" at pizza places, drug stores, diners and on your front porch was a good time. It was a simple, unsophisticated era, but so memorable. The Hometown Club is giving Paul and me a chance to recapture the past.

If you have a special place in your heart for Cleveland's Near West Side, the Hometown Club is for you. People from all walks of life have lived and worked on the Near West Side. It is an area rich in human efforts and accomplishments, and holds fond memories for many.

The Hometown Club will give you a chance to rekindle your enthusiasm about the old neighborhood, as it provides you with history and past memories about the area. If you like, you may want to come back and participate in activities in your old hometown, and maybe meet some old friends.

The club gives you the opportunity to put something back into the area, too. Your contribution will help current residents obtain needed services to better their lives and strengthen the community.

– Carol Sabo